1-2-3 for Windows
The Visual Learning Guide

Watch for these forthcoming titles in this series:

Quicken 3 for Windows: The Visual Learning Guide
WordPerfect for Windows: The Visual Learning Guide

Available Now!

Windows 3.1: The Visual Learning Guide
Excel 4 for Windows: The Visual Learning Guide
Word for Windows 2: The Visual Learning Guide
WordPerfect 6 for DOS: The Visual Learning Guide

How to Order:

Quantity discounts are available from the publisher, Prima Publishing, P.O. Box 1260BK, Rocklin, CA 95677; telephone (916) 786-0426. On your letterhead include information concerning the intended use of the books and the number of books you wish to purchase.

1-2-3 for Windows
The Visual Learning Guide

Grace Joely Beatty, Ph.D.
David C. Gardner, Ph.D.

Prima Publishing
P.O. Box 1260EXC
Rocklin, CA 95677
(916) 786-0426

Library of Congress Catalog Card Number: 93-2333
ISBN: 1-55958-406-8

Executive Editor: Roger Stewart
Managing Editor: Neweleen A. Trebnik
Project Manager: Becky Freeman
Copy Editing: Becky Whitney
Production and Layout: Marian Hartsough Associates
Interior Design: Grace Joely Beatty, S. Linda Beatty, David C. Gardner,
    Laurie Stewart, and Kim Bartusch
Technical Editing: Linda Miles
Cover Design: Page Design, Inc.
Color Separations: Ocean Quigley
Index: Katherine Stimson

Prima Publishing
Rocklin, CA 95677-1260

93 94 95 96 RRD 10 9 8 7 6 5 4 3 2 1

Printed in the United States of America

Acknowledgments

We are deeply indebted to reviewers around the country who gave generously of their time to test every step in the manuscript. Joseph Beatty, Shirley Beatty, David Coburn, Ray Holder, Jeannie Jones, David Sauer, and Margaret Short cannot be thanked enough!

Carolyn Holder and Anne-Barbara Norris are our in-house production team, reviewers, proofreaders, screen capturers, and friends. They, along with Ray Holder and Margaret Short, keep us functioning.

We are personally and professionally delighted to work with everyone at Prima Publishing, especially Roger Stewart, executive editor; Neweleen Trebnik, managing editor; Becky Freeman, project manager; Debbie Parisi, publicity coordinator; Kim Bartusch, exterior production coordinator; and Linda Beatty, interior production coordinator.

Linda Miles, technical editor; Becky Whitney, copy editor, Ocean Quigley, color separator; Marian Hartsough, interior layout; and Paul Page, cover design, contributed immensely to the final product.

Bill Gladstone and Matt Wagner, of Waterside Productions, created the idea for this series. Their faith in us has never wavered.

Joseph and Shirley Beatty made this series possible. We can never repay them.

Asher Shapiro has always been there when we needed him.

Paula Gardner Capaldo and David Capaldo have been terrific. Thanks, Joshua and Jessica, for being such wonderful kids! Our project humorist, Mike Bumgardner, always came through when we needed a boost!

We could not have met the deadlines without the technical support of Ray Holder, our electrical genius; Fred Harper, of Blue Line Communications, Inc., our computer genius; and Lotus' outstanding technical support staff. Thank you all!

Contents at a Glance

CONTENTS

Part V Special Features...............................183

Customize Your Learning

Prima *Visual Learning Guides* are not like any other computer books you have ever seen. They are based on our years in the classroom, our corporate consulting, and our research at Boston University on the best ways to teach technical information to nontechnical learners. Most important, this series is based on the feedback of a panel of reviewers from across the country who range in computer knowledge from "panicked at the thought" to very sophisticated.

This is not an everything-you've-ever-wanted-to-know-about-Lotus 1-2-3-but-didn't-know-enough-to-ask book. It is designed to give you the information you need to perform basic (and some not so basic) functions with confidence and skill. It is a book that our reviewers claim makes it "really easy" for anyone to learn Lotus 1-2-3 quickly.

Each chapter is illustrated with full-color screen shots to guide you through every task. The combination of screens, step-by-step instructions, and pointers makes it impossible for you to get lost or confused as you follow along on your own computer. You can either work through from the beginning to the end or skip around to master the skills you need. If you have a specific goal you want to accomplish now, choose it from the following list.

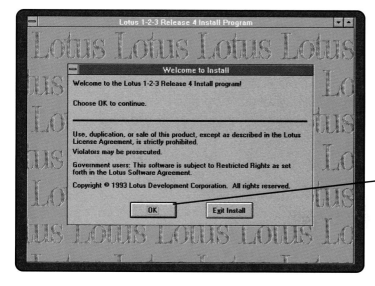

SELECT YOUR GOALS

From the list below, select your personal goals so that you can start using Lotus 1-2-3 immediately.

❖ I would like help installing Lotus 1-2-3 for Windows.

Go to Appendix A.

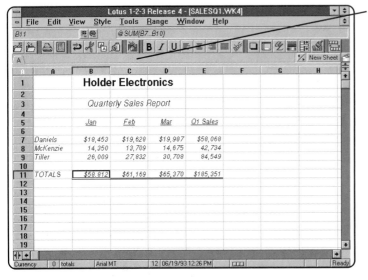

❖ I'm new to Lotus 1-2-3 and I want to learn how to set up a basic worksheet.

Turn to Part I to create a basic worksheet. Go on to Part II to add style to the worksheet.

You can learn how to write formulas in Chapter 13, "Writing Formulas."

❖ I want to learn how to work with multiple worksheets.

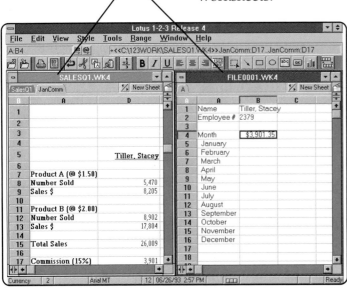

Turn to Part III. In this same part, you can also learn how to link worksheets together so that they share common information.

❖ I want to make a chart to illustrate the information on my worksheet.

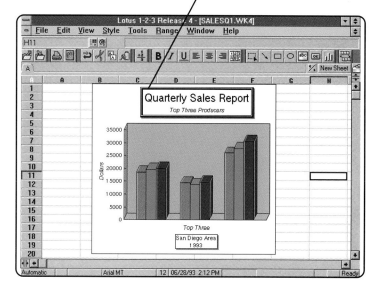

Turn to Chapters 17 and 18.

If you have not developed a worksheet from which to make a chart, go to Part I first.

If you want to add style to your chart by changing fonts and adding arrows, borders, patterns, and text, go on to Chapters 21 and 22.

❖ I want to learn about Dynamic Data Exchange and the linking feature of Lotus 1-2-3 for Windows.

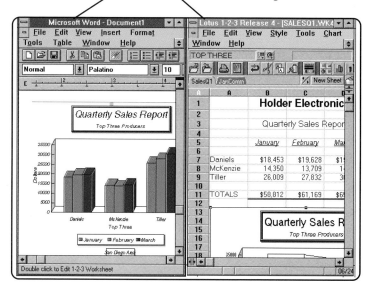

Go to Chapter 23.

Program Manager

Part I: Creating a Basic Worksheet

Setting Up a New Worksheet

This latest version of 1-2-3 makes it especially easy to create a worksheet, format and manipulate data, and take advantage of new features such as in-cell editing, drag-and-drop moving and copying, and context-sensitive quick menus.

1-2-3 Release 4 has a great deal of built-in intelligence. SmartIcons have been programmed to perform many tasks at the click of your mouse. 1-2-3 can complete a series based on a single entry and even sort data after it has been entered. In this chapter, you will do the following:

❖ Create a basic worksheet

❖ Complete a series using a SmartIcon

❖ Sort a column alphabetically

OPENING LOTUS 1-2-3

1. Type win at the **C:\\>(C prompt)** on your screen to boot up Windows if it is not already on your screen. Because Windows provides for tremendous customization, you will probably have different group icons than you see in this example.

2. Click twice quickly on the **Lotus Applications group icon**. It will open up to a window. If you are new to Windows, it may take a little time to get the right rhythm on the double-click. Don't worry if the icon jumps around a little when you click on it.

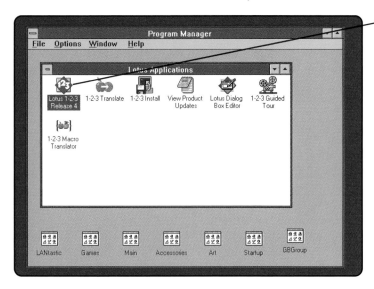

3. **Click twice** on the **Lotus 1-2-3 Release 4 icon**. Your 1-2-3 icon may be in a different spot than you see here. You will see an hourglass and then the copyright information for 1-2-3. Finally, the 1-2-3 opening screen will appear.

INCREASING THE SIZE OF THE 1-2-3 SCREEN

When you open (boot up) 1-2-3 for the first time, your screen may look something like the example to the left. Notice that 1-2-3 does not fill the whole screen. You can increase the size of the Lotus screen very easily.

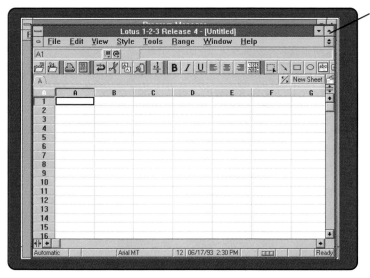

1. **Click** on the **Maximize button (▲)** on the right side of the Lotus 1-2-3 title bar. This will cause 1-2-3 to fill your screen and give you more work space.

THE 1-2-3 WORKSHEET

This is the standard opening screen in Lotus 1-2-3.

Notice that the worksheet is labeled "(Untitled)." This will change when you name the file.

A worksheet is made up of *columns* and *rows*. The intersection of a column and a row forms a block, or *cell*.

The border, or *cell pointer*, around the first cell on the worksheet tells you that this is the *active*, or *current*, cell. This is the cell that will be affected by the next entry or command.

Notice that column heading A and row heading 1 appear depressed to show that A1 is the selected cell.

This is a close-up view of a portion of the screen. You will see both close-up views and full-screen views in this book.

The *cell address* also tells you which cell has been selected to receive the next entry or command. The cell address is A1 because the selected cell is located in column A, row 1.

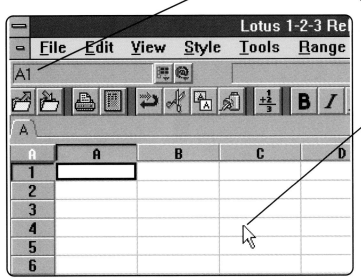

Notice the mouse pointer has an arrow shape when it is in the worksheet area. The pointer changes shape depending on its location and the action you are performing.

ENTERING A WORKSHEET TITLE

When you create a worksheet, it is a good idea to enter a title. After the worksheet is printed, the worksheet title will enable you (and others) to know what the subject is.

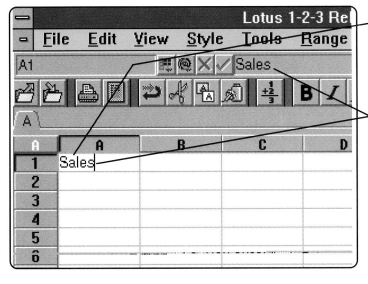

1. **Click** on cell **A1** if it does not already have a border around it. (On your screen it will be blank.)

2. **Type** the word **Sales**. The letters will appear in the cell. They will also appear in the *contents box*, which displays characters as you type. If you make a typing error, just press the Backspace key and retype.

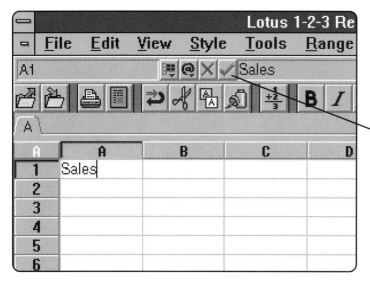

When you begin to type, notice that an X (the *Cancel button*) and a ✔ (the *Confirm button*) appear to the left of the contents box.

3. Click on ✔ to confirm that you want to enter "Sales" into A1. The Cancel and Confirm buttons will disappear after you confirm the entry.

ENTERING COLUMN HEADINGS

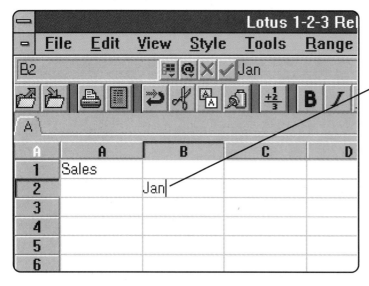

In this section, you will enter the abbreviation for January as the heading for column B.

1. Click on **B2**. On your screen it will be blank.

2. Type Jan. Do not type a period after the abbreviation.

3. Press the **Enter** key on your keyboard. (This does the same thing as clicking on the ✔.)

USING THE FILL BY EXAMPLE FEATURE TO COMPLETE A SERIES

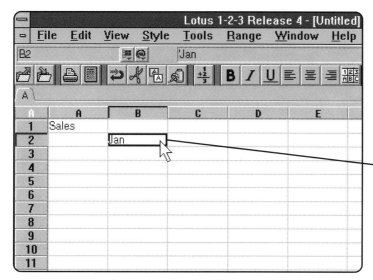

After you have typed the first name in a common series (such as months in the year or days in the week), you can use the Fill By Example feature to complete the series.

1. Move the mouse pointer to **the cell**. (If you see a little hand appear, don't worry. Just move the mouse until you see the arrow again. You will use the hand in "Drag-and-Drop Moving" in Chapter 12.)

2. Press and hold the mouse button as you **drag** the mouse arrow **across columns C and D**. You will see a solid rectangle and a dotted rectangle as you drag the mouse. This symbol indicates that you are selecting a *range*, or a group of adjacent cells.

3. Release the button. The cells will be highlighted.

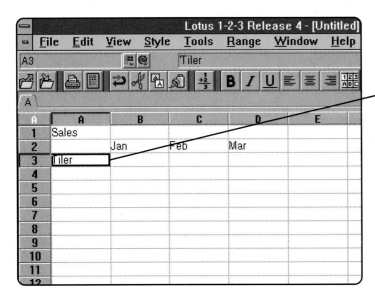

4. Click on the **Fill by Example SmartIcon**.

The series will be completed as shown. If you had typed **Jan.** (with a period), it would not be recognized as the start of a series because 1-2-3 is not set up with a model that has a period after the abbreviation. (Strange, but true.) When Lotus doesn't recognize the first cell in a "Fill By Example" series, it copies the contents of the first cell into all the highlighted cells.

If you mistakenly fill in more cells in the series than you want, simply click on the unwanted cell and press the Delete key.

This procedure works to fill in a series of numbers. You can also use this procedure in rows or columns.

ENTERING ROW HEADINGS

1. Click on **A3**. On your screen, the cell will be blank.

2. Type the name **Tiler**.

3. **Click** on **A4**. On your screen, it will be blank.

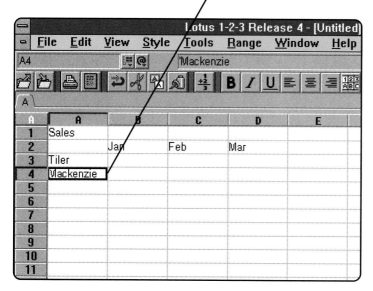

Notice that clicking on another cell automatically enters the data you just typed and moves you to the second cell.

4. **Type** the name **Mackenzie**.

5. **Click** on **A5**. On your screen, it will be blank.

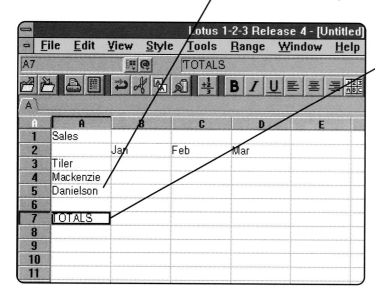

6. **Type** the name **Danielson**.

7. **Click** on **A7**. On your screen, it will be blank.

8. **Type TOTALS**.

9. **Press Enter**, or **click** on ✔.

Your worksheet will look like the example to the left.

SORTING DATA ALPHABETICALLY

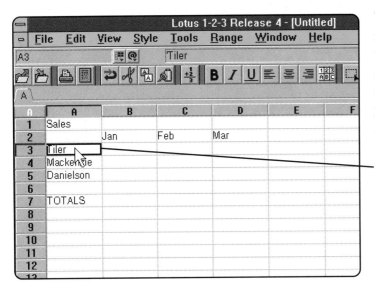

The ability to sort data after it has been entered into the worksheet is a helpful feature of 1-2-3. In this section, you will sort the names in column A alphabetically.

1. Click on **A3** and leave the pointer in the middle of the cell.

2. Press and hold the mouse button and **drag** the pointer down to **A5**.

3. Release the mouse button when you have highlighted the range A3 through A5.

Notice that the range is highlighted in black except for the first cell, which remains white to tell you that this is the active cell.

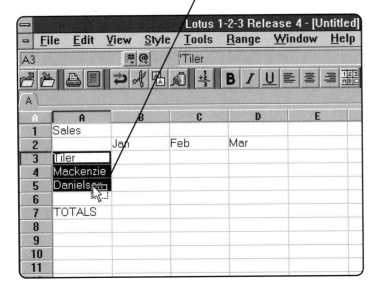

4. Click on **Range** in the menu bar. A pull-down menu will appear.

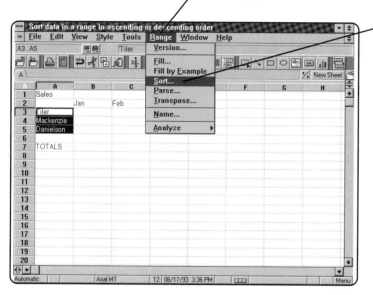

5. Click on **Sort**. Three dots (called an *ellipsis*) after a choice indicate that selecting this choice will bring up a dialog box that will ask for additional information. In this case the Sort dialog box will appear. It's all right if the dialog box appears in a different spot on the screen than the one in the next example.

A3 in the Sort by box shows you where the sort is starting. A3..A5 in the Range box shows you that cells A3 to A5 will be sorted.

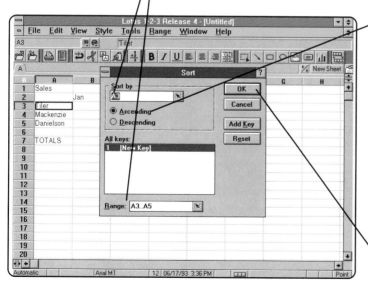

6. Click on **Ascending** if it does not already have a dot in the circle.

Ascending order means sorting from A to Z (or smallest to largest for numbers). *Descending* order means sorting from Z to A (or largest to smallest for numbers).

7. Click on **OK**. The dialog box will disappear.

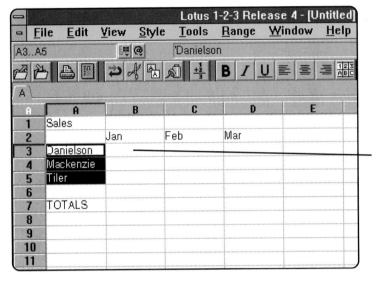

The names are now sorted alphabetically.

ENTERING NUMBERS

1. **Click** on **B3**.

2. **Type** the number **18453**.

3. **Press** the ↓ key on your keyboard to enter the number into B3 and automatically move the selection border to B4. Using the arrow keys on your keyboard is another way to enter data and move around the worksheet. (If you are using the arrows on the numeric keyboard, make sure Num Lock and Scroll Lock are turned off.)

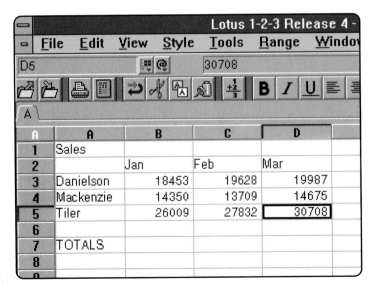

4. **Enter** the **numbers** shown on the screen to the left in the appropriate cells on your worksheet. You can enter the numbers with the arrow keys, by clicking on ✔, or by pressing Enter.

Notice that numbers are aligned on the right in a cell. Text is aligned on the left.

Naming and Saving a File to a Working Directory

It's a good idea to set up what is called a *working directory* for your 1-2-3 files. This way the files you create will remain separate from the files that run 1-2-3. You can easily create a working directory by using File Manager. In this chapter, you will do the following:

❖ Create a working directory

❖ Name a file by using the Save As command

❖ Learn two ways to save a file

CREATING A WORKING DIRECTORY

In this section, you will use File Manager to create a working directory for your 1-2-3 worksheets.

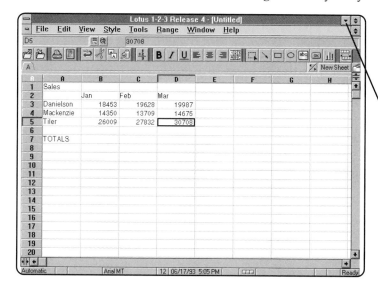

Minimizing 1-2-3

1. **Click** on the **Minimize button** (▼) on the right side of the Lotus 1-2-3 title bar. This will minimize 1-2-3 to an icon at the bottom of your screen.

Sizing Program Manager

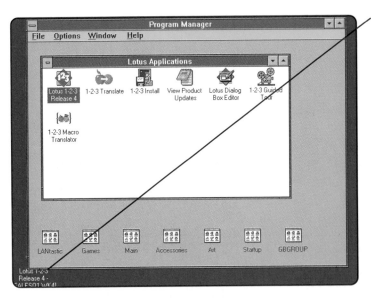

If you cannot see the 1-2-3 icon at the bottom of your screen, complete the following step.

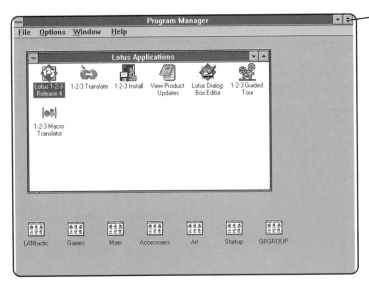

1. Click on the **Restore button** to the right of the Program Manager title bar. (The Restore button is a two-headed arrow that points both up and down.) This will change the size of the Program Manager window so that you can see the minimized 1-2-3 icon.

Opening File Manager

File Manager is usually located in the Main group window. It's possible that your File Manager icon was moved to another group window.

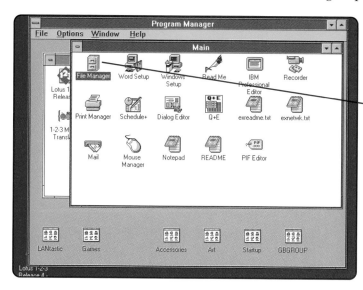

1. **Click twice** on the **Main group icon**. The group will open up to a window.

2. **Click twice** on the **File Manager icon**. (It may be in a different place in your group window than you see here.) The File Manager window will appear on your screen. It may appear in a different location and in a different size than you see in the next example.

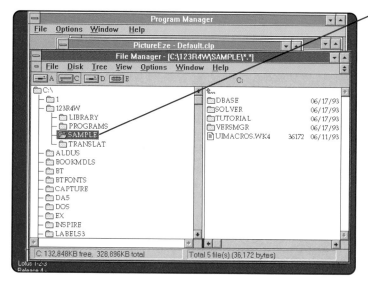

In this example, the Sample directory is highlighted. On your computer, the C:\ or another directory may be highlighted. The contents of File Manager depend on the programs you have installed on your computer. Your list will be different from what you see here.

Changing the View of File Manager

If File Manager does not show a list of files on the right, you can change the view to display the list.

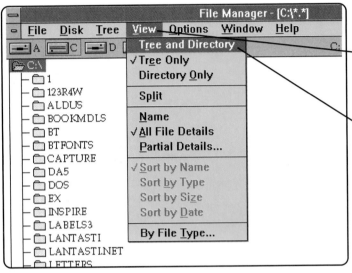

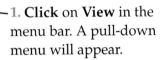

1. **Click** on **View** in the menu bar. A pull-down menu will appear.

2. **Click** on **Tree and Directory**. The list of files in the highlighted directory will appear on the right side of the File Manager window.

Maximizing File Manager

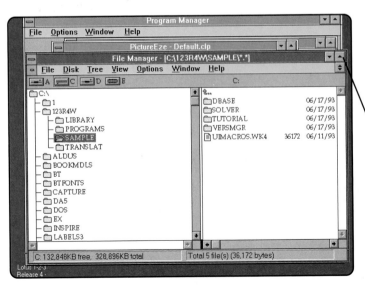

If your File Manager window does not fill the screen, complete the following step.

1. **Click** on the **Maximize button (▲)** on the right side of the File Manager title bar. The File Manager window will be maximized to fill the screen.

Creating a Directory

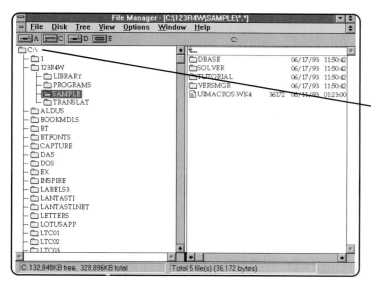

You are now ready to create a directory you will use to store your 1-2-3 worksheet files.

1. Click on **C:** at the top of the directories list. If you cannot see the **C:** at the top of the directory list, do the following.

2. Press the **Home key** on your keyboard. The highlight bar will move to C:\ at the top of the directories list.

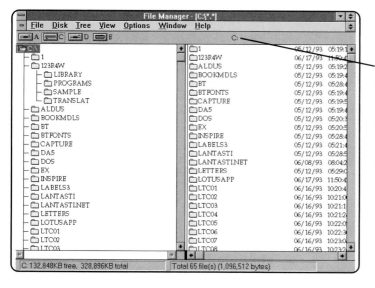

A list of the directories on the C drive will be displayed on the right side of the screen. Your list will be different from what you see here.

3. **Click** on **File** in the menu bar. A pull-down menu will appear.

4. **Click** on **Create Directory**. The Create Directory dialog box will appear.

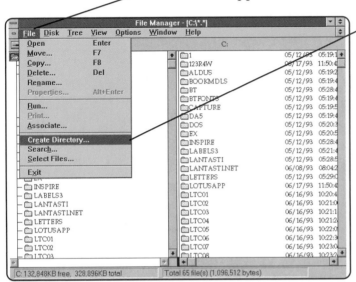

5. Because the cursor is already flashing in the Name box, **type 123work**. You can give this new directory another name if you prefer, but use no more than eight letters in the name.

It doesn't matter whether you type the directory name in upper- or lowercase letters. File Manager will automatically show the directory name in uppercase letters when it appears in the directory list.

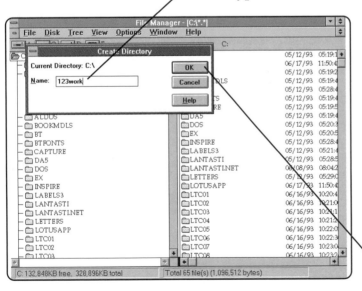

6. **Click** on **OK**. The dialog box will close.

Checking the New Directory and Closing File Manager

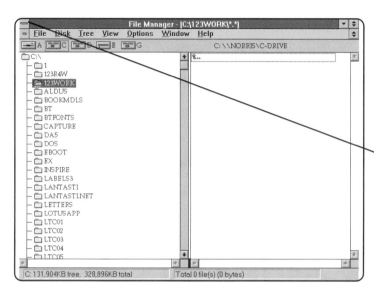

1. Click on **123WORK** in the directory list to highlight it. Notice that there are no files listed on the right. This is because you have not saved any files to this directory.

2. Click twice on the **top Control menu box** (⊟) to the left of the File Manager title bar. This will close File Manager.

Returning to 1-2-3

1. Click twice on the Main Group **Control menu box** (⊟). The Main group window will close. You will see the Lotus Applications group window on your screen.

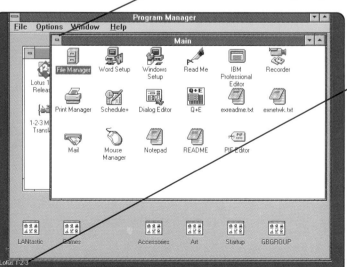

2. Click twice on the **1-2-3 icon** at the bottom of your screen. 1-2-3 will be restored to a window. You will be exactly where you were when you minimized the program.

SETTING THE WORKING DIRECTORY IN 1-2-3

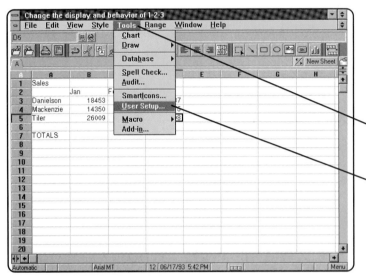

Although you have created the working directory in File Manager, 1-2-3 needs to be told to save your files to this new directory

1. **Click** on **Tools**. A pull-down menu will appear.

2. **Click** on **User Setup**. The User Setup dialog box will appear.

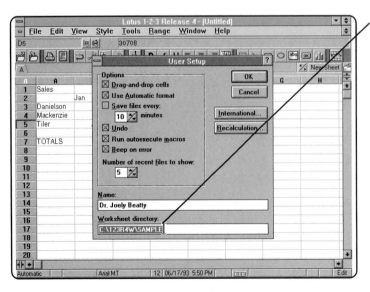

3. **Click twice** on the **Worksheet directory box**. C:\123R4W\SAMPLE will be highlighted.

4. **Type C:\123work**. It will replace the highlighted text.

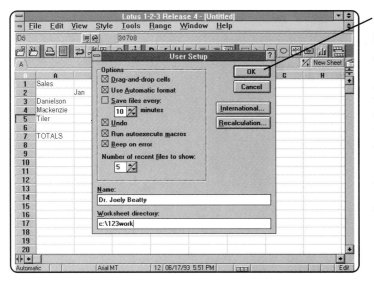

5. **Click** on **OK**. The User Setup dialog box will disappear.

From now on, 123work will automatically come up as the directory to which your work will be saved.

You are now ready to name and save the worksheet.

USING THE SAVE SmartIcon

In this section, you will use the Save SmartIcon to name and save the worksheet you created in Chapter 1.

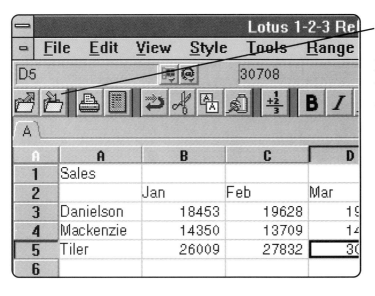

1. **Click** on the **Save SmartIcon**. Because you have not named the file yet, the Save As dialog box will appear.

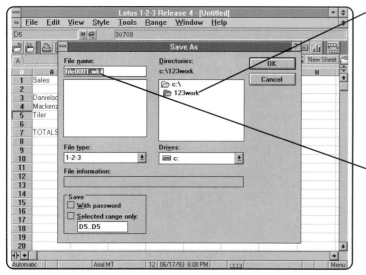

Notice that the 123work directory is already selected. The open file folders next to c:\ and 123work indicate that the file will be saved on the C drive in the 123work directory.

Because file0001.wk4 in the File name text box is already highlighted, you can simply begin to type the new filename.

2. **Type salesq1.** (Filenames are not allowed to have spaces). It will replace the highlighted text.

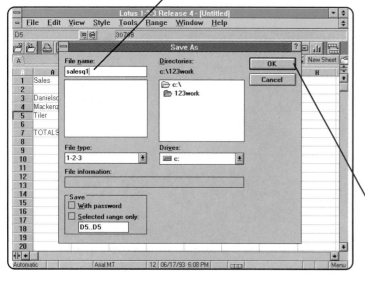

It doesn't matter if you type the filename in upper- or lowercase letters. The filename will appear in uppercase letters on the worksheet. Lotus 1-2-3 will automatically add the .WK4 extension to identify it as a worksheet in Release 4.

3. **Click** on **OK**. You will be returned to the SALESQ1.WK4 worksheet.

SAVING A FILE WITH THE SAVE SmartIcon

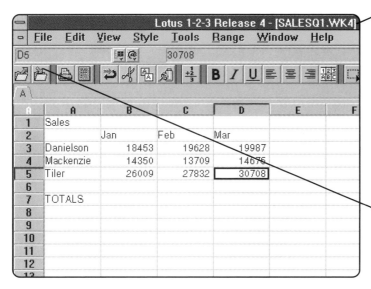

Notice the filename at the top of your worksheet.

Develop the habit of saving your file while you work on it. Save often. This will spare you much grief and aggravation in the event of a power failure or equipment problem.

1. **Click** on the **Save SmartIcon**. An hourglass will appear very briefly. Your worksheet is now saved. Do this often.

CHECKING A SmartIcon

If you want to check whether a SmartIcon is the correct one to use, use this handy feature of 1-2-3.

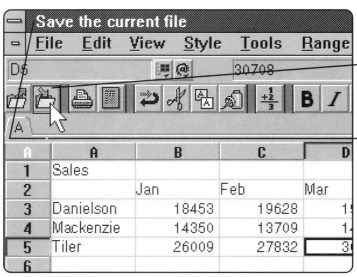

1. **Place** (*don't click*) the mouse pointer on top of the **Save SmartIcon**.

2. **Press and hold** the *right mouse button*. You will see a description of the SmartIcon function at the top of your screen.

Editing Your Worksheet

Editing is straightforward in 1-2-3 because of one of Lotus' newest features, in-cell editing, which allows you to edit the contents of a cell directly in the cell. Using the mouse gives you a great deal of control in the editing process. You can change the contents of a cell, change individual letters or numbers in a cell, clear a cell completely, or even undo your edit if you change your mind. In this chapter, you will do the following:

❖ Make edits to the worksheet you created in Chapter 1 so that you can use the worksheet throughout the rest of this book

❖ Cancel an edit

❖ Use the Undo SmartIcon

ADDING DATA

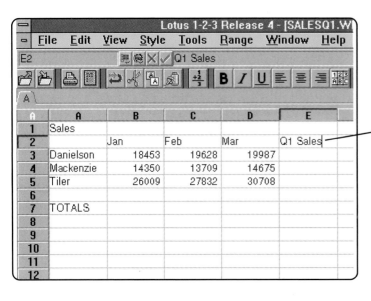

You can add data at any time to a worksheet. In this section, you will add the heading "Q1 Sales" to Column E.

1. Click on **E2**. On your screen, it will be blank.

2. Type Q1 Sales and **press Enter**.

INSERTING A CHARACTER INTO A CELL

In this section, you will change the name "Tiler" to "Tiller" with in-cell editing.

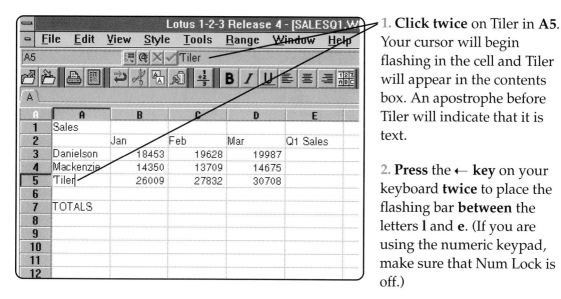

1. **Click twice** on Tiler in **A5**. Your cursor will begin flashing in the cell and Tiler will appear in the contents box. An apostrophe before Tiler will indicate that it is text.

2. **Press** the ← **key** on your keyboard **twice** to place the flashing bar **between** the letters **l** and **e**. (If you are using the numeric keypad, make sure that Num Lock is off.)

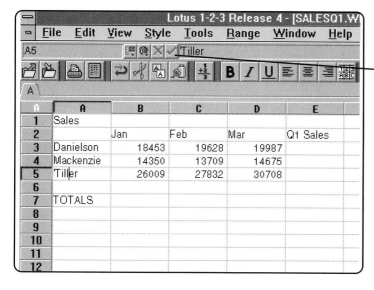

3. **Type** the letter l. It will be added to the name.

4. **Click** on ✔ or press Enter to enter the change in the cell.

DELETING A CHARACTER FROM A CELL

In this section, you will change the name "Mackenzie" to McKenzie."

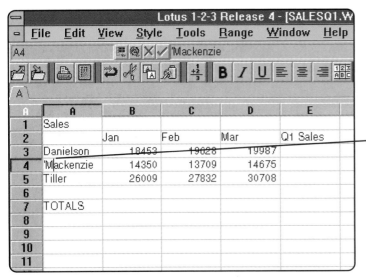

Deleting to the Right

1. Click twice on Mackenzie in **A4**.

2. Place the mouse pointer between the letters **M** and **a**. The pointer will change to an I-beam.

3. Click to set the cursor in place. It will change to a flashing bar.

4. Press the **Delete** key to delete the letter "a."

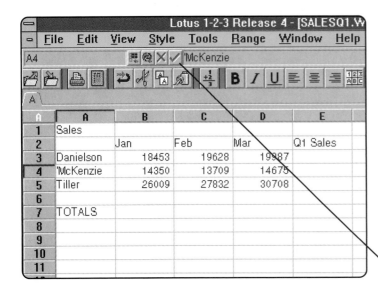

Deleting to the Left

1. Press → twice to move the flashing bar to the right of the letter "k."

2. Press the **Backspace** key to delete the "k."

3. Type a capital **K** to make the name McKenzie.

4. Click on ✔ or press Enter.

DELETING MORE THAN ONE CHARACTER

You can edit the contents of a cell in the contents box. In this section, you will change the name "Danielson" to "Daniels."

1. **Click once** on Danielson in **A3**.

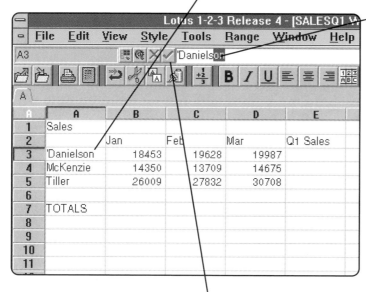

2. **Move** the mouse pointer up to the contents box and **place** it at the **end** of the **word**. The pointer will change to an I-beam.

3. **Press and hold** the mouse button as you **drag** the highlight bar over the **last two letters** in the name.

4. **Release** the mouse button.

5. **Press Backspace** to delete the letters.

6. **Click** on ✔ or press Enter to confirm the change.

CANCELING AN EDIT

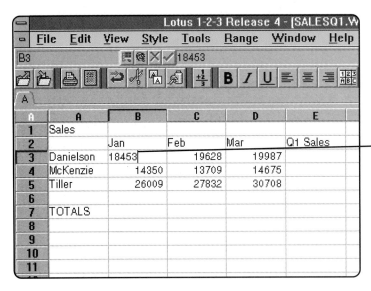

If you're like the rest of us, you occasionally make a change you didn't intend to make. If you catch the mistake before you confirm the change, you can undo it.

1. Click twice on **B3**. Notice that the number appears at the left of the cell.

2. Place the **cursor** at the **beginning** of the number. the cursor will change to an I-beam.

3. Click the mouse button **twice**. The contents of the cell will be highlighted.

4. Type the number **20000**. It will replace the highlighted number. (Do *not* press Enter.)

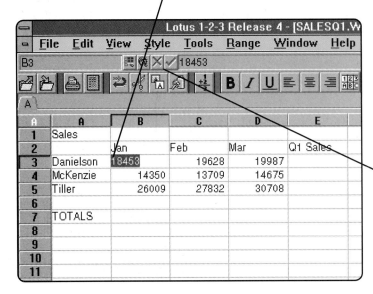

At this point, you discover that you should not have changed the number. Because you are still in the cell and you have not pressed Enter, you can simply cancel the change.

5. Click on ✕ (the Cancel button) in the edit bar to undo the change. The original number, 18453, will appear again.

USING THE UNDO SmartIcon

If you actually enter a change and then decide you don't want it, you can undo the change with the Undo SmartIcon as long as you use it before you perform any other function.

In this section, you will clear the contents of a cell and then undo the change.

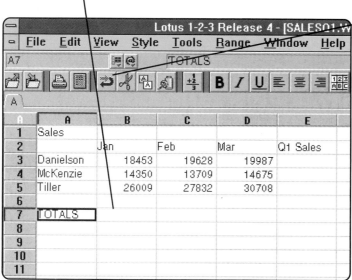

1. **Click** once on TOTALS in **A7**.

2. **Press** the **Delete key**. The contents of the cell will be cleared.

3. **Click** on **B7**.

4. **Click** on the **Undo Smart-Icon**. The contents of **A7** will be restored. Even though you moved to a new cell, you did not perform an actual function such as entering data or using a menu bar command. Therefore, you can use the Undo SmartIcon.

A general rule of thumb is that you can use the ✕ (Cancel button) when it is visible. If it is not visible, use the Undo SmartIcon.

Totaling Columns and Rows

This is the fun part! Lotus has a wonderful icon that contains a built-in formula to total columns and rows. You can then use other features, such as Fill by Example, Edit Copy Down, and Edit Copy Right to copy the addition formula to adjacent cells. In this chapter, you will do the following:

❖ Use the Addition SmartIcon to total columns and rows

❖ Use the Fill by Example feature to copy the addition formula to other cells

❖ Use the Edit Copy Right command to copy a formula to adjacent cells

USING THE ADDITION SMARTICON

Although you can write a formula to total a column or row, clicking on the Addition SmartIcon creates the formula for you automatically. (You will learn how to write formulas in Chapter 13, "Writing Formulas.")

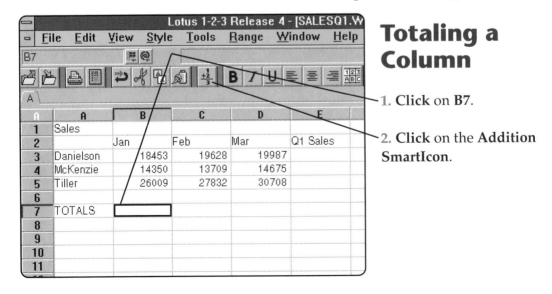

Totaling a Column

1. **Click** on **B7**.

2. **Click** on the **Addition SmartIcon**.

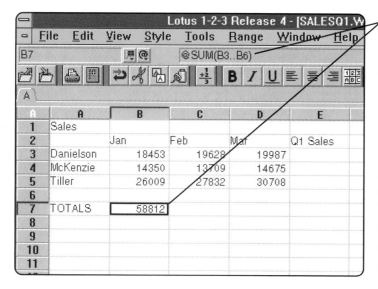

The formula for summing the column, SUM(B3..B6), will appear in the contents box, and the sum (58812) will immediately appear in B7.

Don't get carried away by your enthusiasm and add columns C and D just yet. You will learn how to copy the sum formula to other columns a little later in the chapter.

Totaling a Row

1. Click on **E3**.

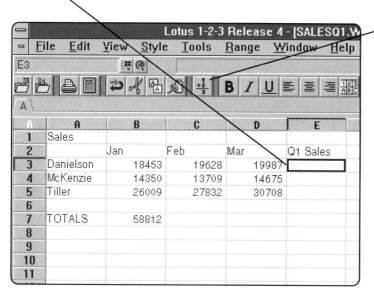

2. Click on the **Addition SmartIcon**, and the total of row 3 (58068) will appear in E3.

COPYING A FORMULA USING THE FILL BY EXAMPLE
SmartIcon

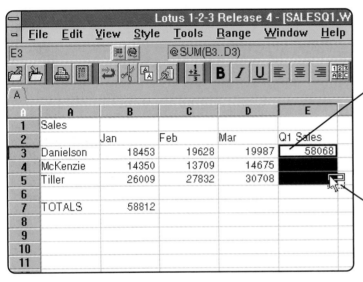

You can copy a formula to adjacent cells with the Fill By Example SmartIcon.

1. Click on **E3**, the cell you want to copy. If you have been following these procedures, it is already selected.

2. Press and hold the mouse button and **drag** the arrow down to **E4** and **E5**. The cells will be highlighted.

Do not extend the highlighting down to E7. Because there are no numbers in row 6 to total, the formula will put a 0 in cell E6. You will include E7 in the next step.

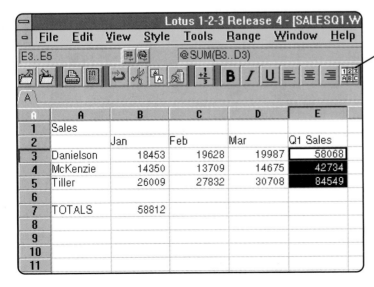

3. Release the mouse button.

4. Click on the **Fill By Example SmartIcon**.

The sum of row 4 (42734) will appear in E4, and the sum of row 5 (84549) will appear in E5.

COPYING A FORMULA WITH THE EDIT COPY RIGHT COMMAND

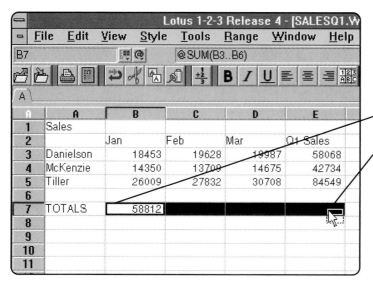

Using the Edit Copy Right command is another way to copy a formula to adjacent cells.

1. **Click** on **B7**.

2. **Press and hold** the mouse button and **drag** the arrow across the row to **E7**.

3. **Release** the mouse button.

4. **Click** on **Edit** in the **menu bar**. A pull-down menu will appear.

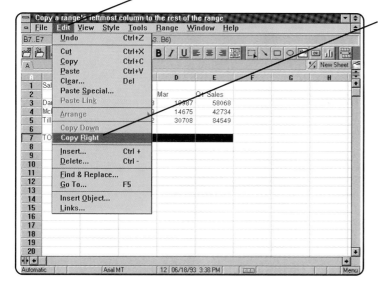

5. **Click** on **Copy Right**.

Notice on the Edit pull-down menu that there is also a Copy Down command which is used to copy within a column.

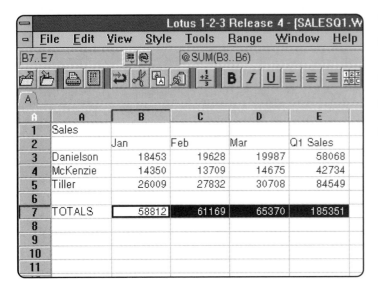

The following sums will appear:

Column C = 61169

Column D = 65370

Column E = 185351

SAVING WITH THE SAVE SmartIcon

Once again, it's a good idea to save frequently.

1. **Click** on the **Save SmartIcon**. The changes you made will be saved to C:\123WORK\SALESQ1.WK4.

2. **Click anywhere** else on your **worksheet** to remove the highlight bar.

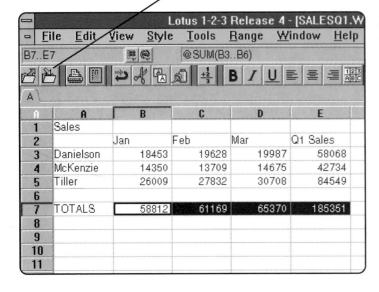

Using Page Setup and Print Preview, and Printing a File

When you print a 1-2-3 file, you can customize the printed page in a number of ways. For example, you can add identifying information to a file with headers and footers. You can increase the size of the printed worksheet. You can print the gridlines you see on your screen. You can even preview a file to see what it will look like before it prints. In this chapter, you will do the following:

❖ Print the worksheet

❖ Use the Page Setup options

❖ Add a header to a file

❖ Use the preview feature

USING THE PRINT SMARTICON

1. **Click** on the **Print SmartIcon**. The Print dialog box will appear.

	Lotus 1-2-3 Release 4 - [SALESQ1.W

File Edit View Style Tools Range Window Help

H20

A				
	A	**B**	**C**	**D**	**E**
1	Sales				
2		Jan	Feb	Mar	Q1 Sales
3	Danielson	18453	19628	19987	58068
4	McKenzie	14350	13709	14675	42734
5	Tiller	26009	27832	30708	84549
6					
7	TOTALS	58812	61169	65370	185351
8					
9					
10					
11					

2. Click on **Current worksheet** if it does not already have a dot in the circle.

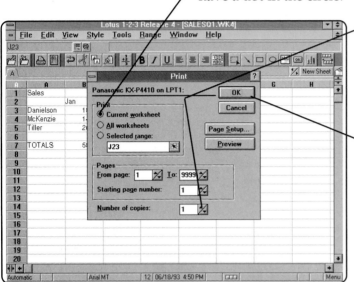

Notice that you can increase the number of copies to be printed by clicking on the up arrow in the Number of copies box.

3. Click on **OK**. Your worksheet will print and you will be returned to the worksheet screen.

USING PAGE SETUP OPTIONS

You can customize many features of printing in 1-2-3. The settings you make in the Page Setup dialog box affect only this particular file.

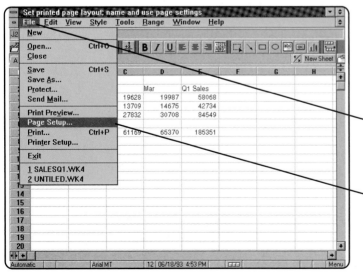

Opening the Page Setup Dialog Box

1. Click on **File** in the menu bar. A pull-down list will appear.

2. Click on **Page Setup**. The Page Setup dialog box will appear.

Using Grid Lines

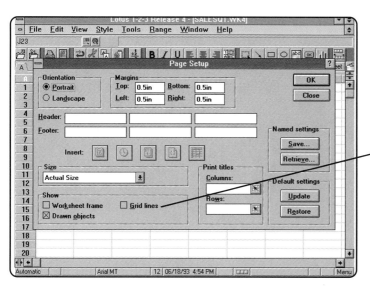

1-2-3 is set up so that the grid lines do not show on the printed page. If you want the grid lines to show on the printed page, do the following.

1. **Click** on **Grid lines** to insert an X in the box. This means that this feature is now selected. To remove this selected feature, simply click on Grid lines again to remove the X.

Inserting A Header

A header is a line of type added to the top of the printed page. It usually contains identifying data, such as the filename or the date, but it can be any text you want. A header can be aligned with the left margin, centered, or aligned with the right margin.

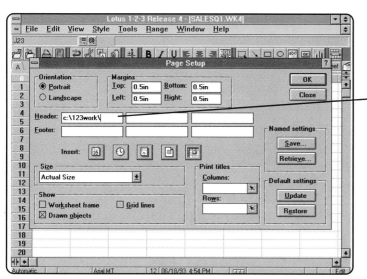

1. **Click** on the **left header box**. Your cursor will flash in the box and the grayed-out (inactive) icons below the Footer boxes will now be brightly colored and active.

2. **Type c:\123work\.** (Don't include the period.)

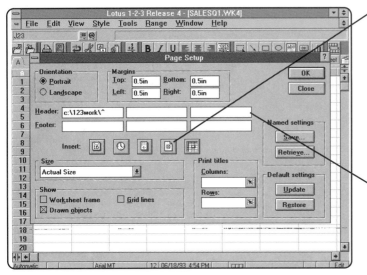

3. Click on the **filename icon**. A caret (^) will appear at the end of C:\123work\. The ^ is the symbol 1-2-3 uses to represent the filename. When you print, the filename will be printed instead of the ^.

4. Click on the **right header box**. Your cursor will flash in the box.

5. Click on the **date icon**. An at sign (@) will be inserted into the box. The current date will be printed on the worksheet page. This date will change as you print on different days.

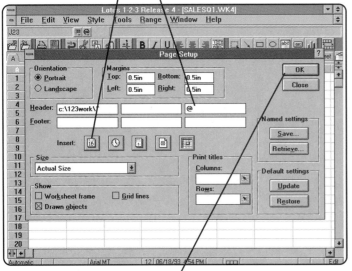

The other icons in this dialog box insert the following information:

🕐 Time of printing

🔢 Page number

⊞ Contents of a cell. After you click on this icon, type the address of the cell that contains what you want to appear in the header.

6. **Click** on **OK**. The Page Setup dialog box will disappear.

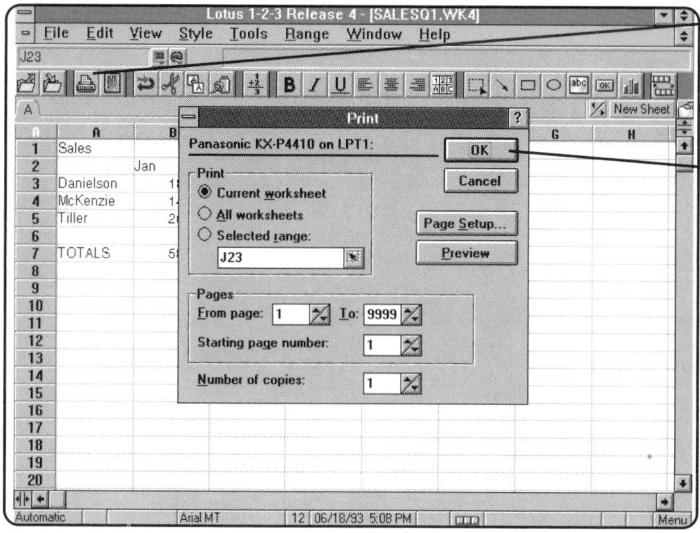

7. **Click** on the **Print SmartIcon**. The Print dialog box will appear.

8. **Click** on **OK** to print the worksheet with the header.

INCREASING THE SIZE OF THE PRINTED WORKSHEET

You can significantly enlarge the size of the worksheet on the printed page. This is especially helpful if you plan to use the page in a presentation.

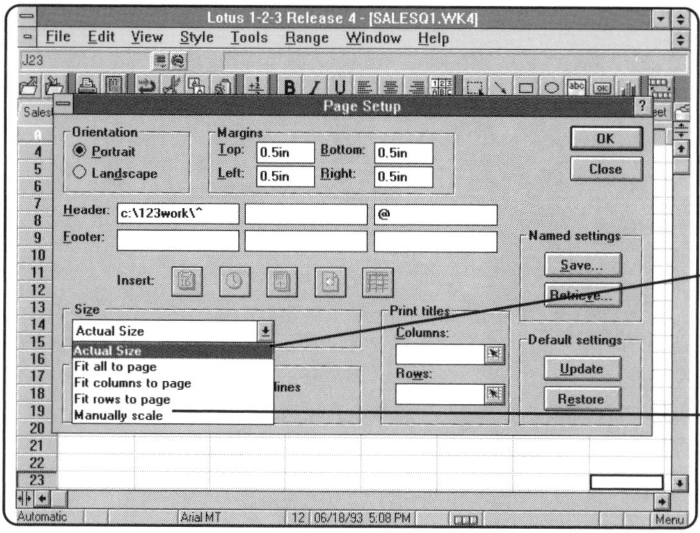

1. **Open** the **Page Setup dialog box**. Refer to the section "Opening the Page Setup Dialog Box" on the second page of this chapter if you need help.

2. **Click** on ⬇ in the Size box. A drop-down list of sizing options will appear.

3. **Click** on **Manually scale**. The list will disappear and a percent box will appear to the right of the size box.

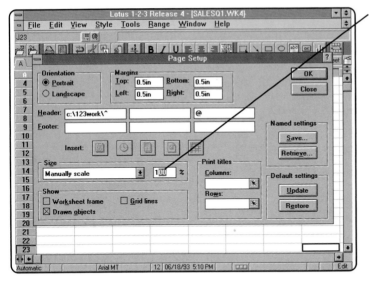

4. Click to the **right of "100"** in the percent box to set the cursor.

5. Press and hold the mouse button and **drag** the cursor over the 00 in 100. The 0s will be highlighted. Release the mouse button.

6. Type 50 to make the enlargement factor 150%. You are able to use such a big enlargement factor because SALESQ1.WK4 doesn't have a lot of data in it. Experiment with different sizes. If you want a smaller print size than normal, type a number less than 100. (This affects the printout only. To change the size of the type on your printout and on the screen, see the section "Increasing Type Size" in Chapter 9.)

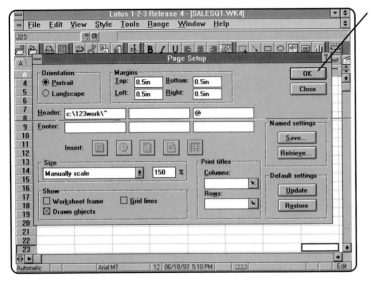

7. Click on **OK**. You will return to your worksheet screen.

PREVIEWING THE PAGE

1. Click on the **Preview SmartIcon**. The Print Preview dialog box will appear.

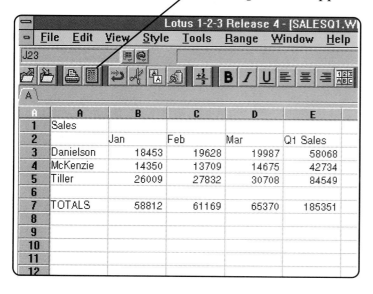

2. Click on **OK**. The Preview screen will appear.

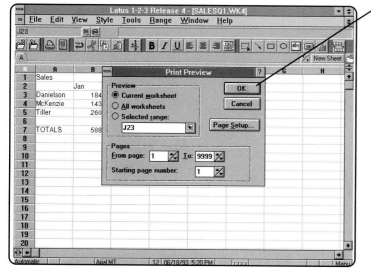

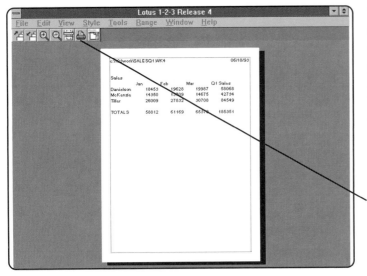

The Preview screen lets you see the placement of the worksheet on the page and make changes before you print.

You can edit the placement of the margins from print preview.

3. **Click** on the **Page Setup SmartIcon**. The Page Setup dialog box will appear.

CHANGING MARGINS THROUGH THE PREVIEW SCREEN

1. **Click twice** in the **Top Margin box**. The contents of the box will be highlighted.

2. **Type 2**.

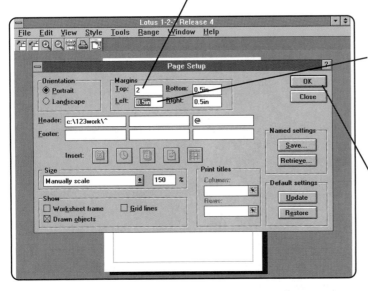

3. **Click twice** in the **Left Margin box**. The contents of the box will be highlighted.

4. **Type 1**.

5. **Click** on **OK**. The preview screen will appear with the change.

RESTORING THE ORIGINAL PAGE SETTINGS

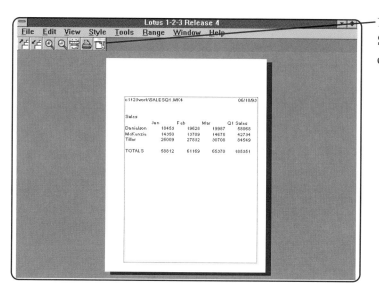

1. **Click** on the **Page Setup SmartIcon**. The Page Setup dialog box will appear.

2. **Click** on **Restore** in the Default settings box. The original Page Setup settings will be restored. This will erase the headers, the changes to the top and left margins, and the scaling change. The examples in the book will show the original page settings.

3. **Click** on **OK**. You will be returned to the Preview screen.

4. **Click anywhere** on the **Preview** screen. You will be returned to your worksheet.

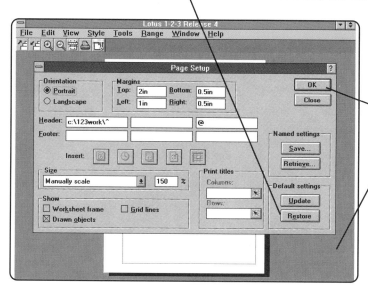

Closing a File and Exiting 1-2-3

In Windows-based programs, you can often accomplish the same task in several different ways. 1-2-3 is no exception. In this chapter, you will:

❖ Learn a quick way to close a file
❖ Learn a quick way to exit 1-2-3

CLOSING A FILE

When you close a file, you do not exit 1-2-3. A new, untitled worksheet appears on your screen.

1. Click twice on the **Control menu box** (⊟) on the left side of the menu bar. Be careful not to click on the *top* Control menu box in the title bar. This will close 1-2-3. If you saved just prior to clicking on the Control menu box, the SALESQ1.WK4 file will close and a new, untitled worksheet will be on your screen.

If you did not save before clicking on the Control menu box, a dialog box will appear and ask if you want to save.

2. Click on **Yes**.

If you click on No, any changes you made to the file since the last time you saved will be lost. If you click on Cancel, the Close dialog box will disappear and you will be returned to the worksheet.

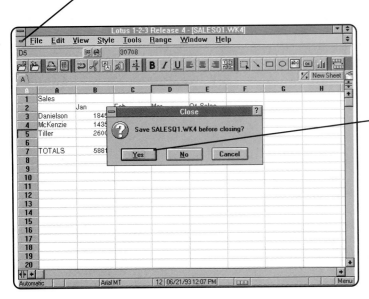

EXITING 1-2-3

If you have been following along with the steps in this chapter, you closed the SALESQ1.WK4 worksheet and you have a blank, untitled worksheet on your screen. If you did not close the file on your screen, this exit procedure will work anyway.

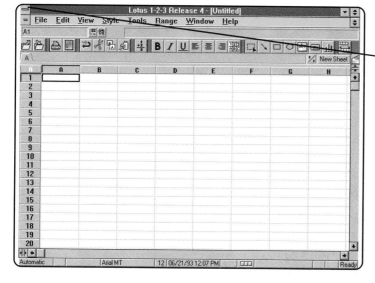
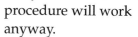

1. **Click twice** on the **Control menu box** (⊟) on the left side of the 1-2-3 title bar. If you saved before doing this, 1-2-3 will close.

If you forgot to save, 1-2-3 will rescue you and ask if you want to save.

2. **Click** on **Yes** to save and exit 1-2-3.

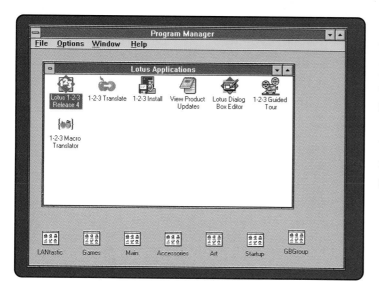

OPENING 1-2-3

If you want to continue to Chapter 7, "Opening a Saved File," reopen 1-2-3.

1. **Click twice** on the **1-2-3 icon**. The 1-2-3 opening screen will appear.

Program Manager

Part II: Adding Style to Your Worksheet

Opening a Saved File

1-2-3 makes opening a saved file as easy as clicking your mouse. In this chapter, you will do the following:

❖ Open the SALESQ1.WK4 file using the File pull-down menu
❖ Open the SALESQ1.WK4 file using a SmartIcon

OPENING A SAVED FILE

1-2-3 has added a special feature to the file pull-down menu that makes opening a saved file especially easy.

Method #1

1. **Click** on **File** in the menu bar. A pull-down menu will appear.

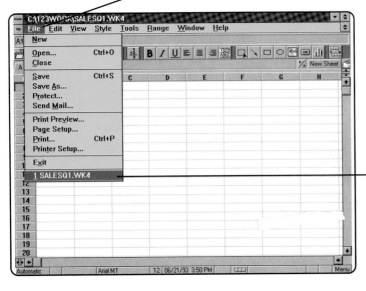

The File pull-down menu lists the five most recent files you have opened. As you create files, the list will change. In this example, SALESQ1.WK4 is the only file on the pull-down menu.

2. **Click** on **SALESQ1.WK4**. The worksheet will appear.

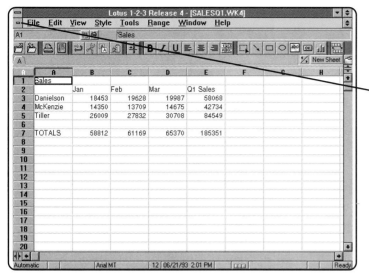

If you want to try method #2, you need to close SALESQ1.WK4 first.

3. Click twice on the **Control menu box** (⊟) in the menu bar. SALESQ1.WK4 will close.

Method #2

1-2-3 has a SmartIcon that makes locating and opening a file especially easy.

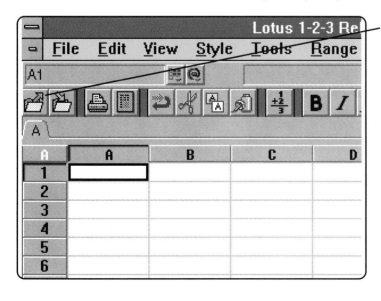

1. Click on the **Open SmartIcon**. The Open file dialog box will appear.

2. Click twice on **SALESQ1.WK4**. The SALESQ1.WK4 worksheet will open.

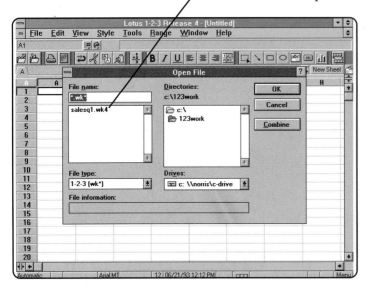

Adding and Deleting Rows

As part of the process of adding and deleting rows, you will use a feature of 1-2-3 called a quick menu. If you think that clicking on the menu bar and getting a pull-down menu is easy, just wait until you use a quick menu! In this chapter, you will do the following:

❖ Add rows

❖ Delete a row

❖ Use a quick menu

ADDING ROWS

Suppose you want the company name on the SALESQ1.WK4 worksheet for a presentation tomorrow. In this section, you will add three rows at the beginning of the SALESQ1.WK4 worksheet so that you can add the company name. You will also add some other blank rows within the worksheet.

Using a Quick Menu

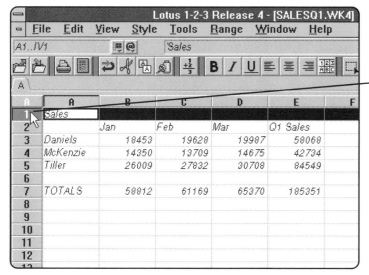

1. **Click** on the **row 1 button**. The entire row will be highlighted. Leave the mouse arrow on the row.

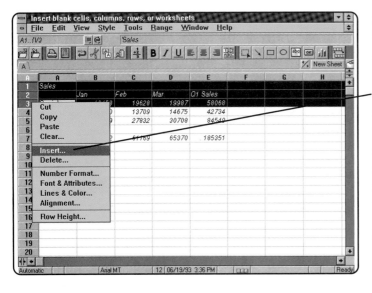

2. Press and hold the mouse button and **drag** the highlight bar down to **row 3**. *Leave the mouse pointer in the highlighted area.* When you are getting ready to use a quick menu, it's important that you leave the mouse pointer in the highlighted area or the next step won't work.

3. Click on the **right** mouse button. A quick menu will appear.

4. Click on **Insert**. Three rows will be inserted at the top of the worksheet. All following rows will be renumbered. 1-2-3 knew to insert rows because you used the row buttons to select the number of rows to be added.

5. **Click** on the **row 5** button. The entire row will be highlighted. Leave the pointer in the cell.

6. **Click** the **right** mouse button. A quick menu will appear.

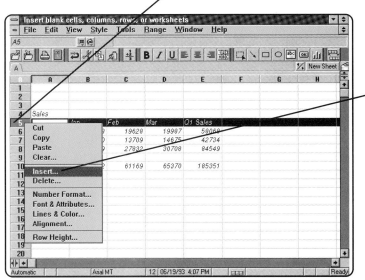

7. **Click** on **Insert**. A row will be inserted at the cursor point. All following rows will be renumbered.

Using the Edit Menu

In this example, you will add a row above the names by using the Edit pull-down menu.

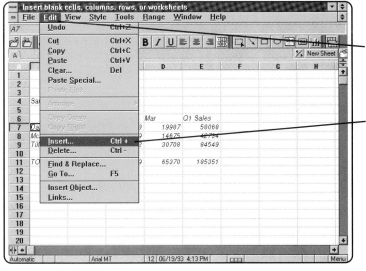

1. **Click** on Daniels in **A7**.

2. **Click** on **Edit** in the menu bar. A pull-down menu will appear.

3. **Click** on **Insert**. The Insert dialog box will appear.

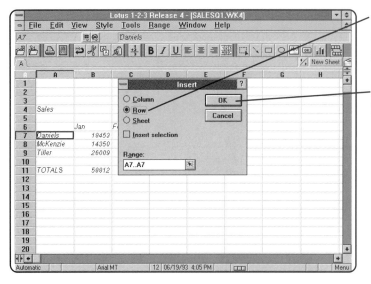

4. Click on **Row** to insert a dot in the circle if one is not already there.

5. Click on **OK**. A row will be added to the worksheet.

DELETING A ROW

After looking at your worksheet, you decide that three rows at the top are too many. Don't worry. Deleting is easy.

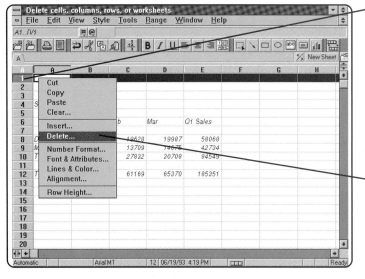

1. Click on the **row 1 button**. This will select the entire row. *Leave the pointer in the row.*

2. Click the **right** mouse button. A quick menu will appear.

3. Click on **Delete**. The highlighted row will be deleted and its number assigned to the next row.

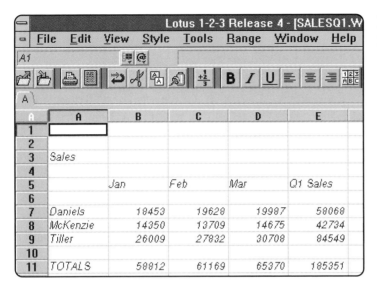

Your worksheet will look like this example.

ADDING A WORKSHEET HEADING

In this section, you will add the company name to the worksheet and change "Sales" to a more descriptive heading.

1. **Click** on **A1**. On your screen, the cell will be empty.

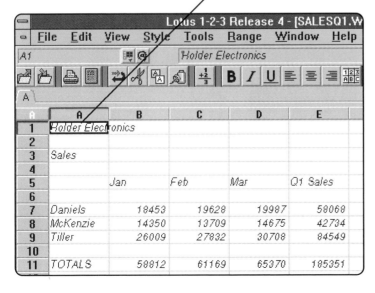

2. **Type Holder Electronics**. Don't be concerned that the name is too long for the cell. As long as the cell to the right is empty, the entry will expand into the next cell.

3. **Press Enter** to insert the name into A1. You will center the company name over the worksheet in the section "Centering Across Columns and Within Cells" in Chapter 9.

4. Click twice on Sales in **A3** to activate the cell for in-cell editing.

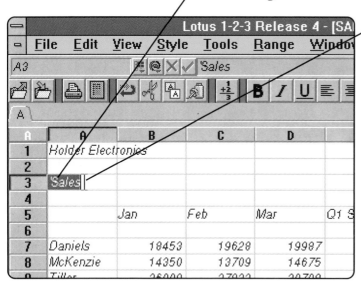

5. With the I-beam in the cell, **click twice**. The contents of the cell will be highlighted.

6. Type the words **Quarterly Sales Report**. They will replace the highlighted text.

7. Press Enter to insert "Quarterly Sales Report" in A3.

8. Click on the **Save SmartIcon** to save the changes in your worksheet.

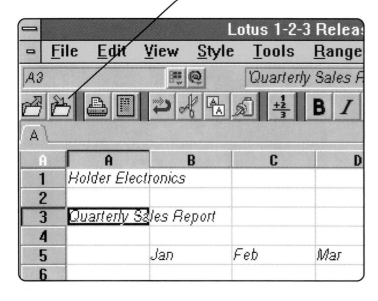

In the next chapter, you will dress up the worksheet with larger type, boldface print, and other style changes.

Formatting the Worksheet and Changing SmartIcons

The SmartIcons you see on your screen are part of the Default SmartIcon set, which contains icons for the most commonly performed tasks. 1-2-3 has sets of specialized SmartIcons. One of these sets, the Formatting set, contains icons to help you improve the appearance of your worksheet. In this chapter, you will do the following:

❖ Change the SmartIcons

❖ Increase the type size

❖ Change the type style to bold, italic, and underline

❖ Add a border to a cell

❖ Center text across columns and within cells

CHANGING THE SmartIcons

1. Click on the **SmartIcons** buttons in the status bar at the bottom of the worksheet. A pop-up list of SmartIcon sets will appear.

2. **Click** on **Formatting**. The SmartIcons on the right side of the SmartIcon bar will change.

INCREASING TYPE SIZE

Notice the Formatting SmartIcons on the right side of the icon palette.

You will learn two ways to increase type size in the following examples.

Using the Status Bar

The status bar at the bottom of your screen allows you to format numbers and text at the click of your mouse. First, select the cell you want to format.

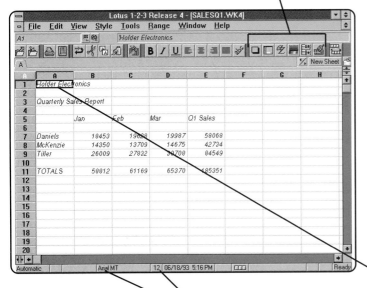

1. Click on Holder Electronics in **A1**.

Notice that the status bar shows Ariel MT as the font and the size as 12 points.

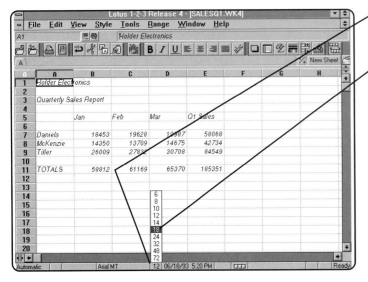

2. Click on **12**. A pop-up list of type sizes will appear.

3. Click on **18** to increase the type size of the selected text to 18 points. You will see the change almost immediately on your screen.

A Note About Appearances

Even though "Holder Electronics" appears to extend into cell B1, 1-2-3 considers it to be in cell A1. Therefore, when you click on A1, both words show in the edit line. Try clicking on cell B1. Notice that nothing shows in the edit line because nothing was actually entered into cell B1. Interesting . . .

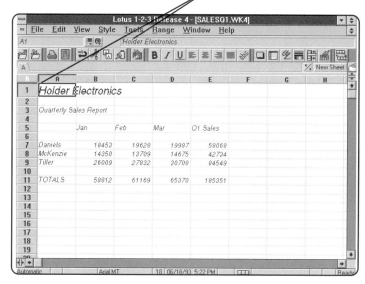

Using a SmartIcon

In this example, you will use the Font & Attributes SmartIcon on the Formatting set. First, select the cell or range you want to format.

1. Click on Quarterly Sales Report in **A3**.

2. Click on the **Font & Attributes SmartIcon**. The Font & Attributes dialog box will appear.

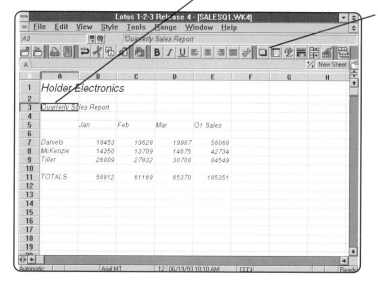

Notice that you can change the font and appearance of text or numbers in this dialog box. You can even underline the contents of a cell.

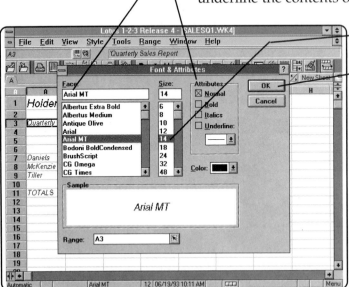

3. Click on **14** in the Size list.

4. Click on **OK**. The dialog box will close and the text will increase to 14 points.

ADDING AND REMOVING BOLDFACE FROM TYPE

Many SmartIcons work like toggle switches. Click to turn the function on, and then click again to turn it off. In this section, you will make text bold, then turn off the boldface, and then turn it on again. First, select the cell you want to change.

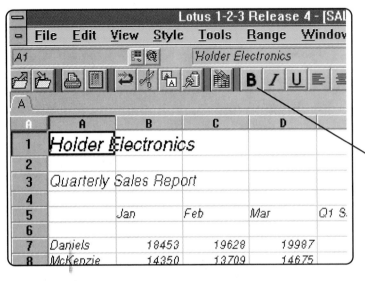

1. Click on Holder Electronics in **A1**.

2. Click on the **Bold SmartIcon** (the large B). The text in A1 will be made bold.

3. Click on the **Bold SmartIcon** again to make the type normal.

4. Click on the **SmartIcon** again to make the text boldface once more.

MAKING TEXT ITALIC

In this section, you will highlight a range and, with one command, apply italics to the entire range.

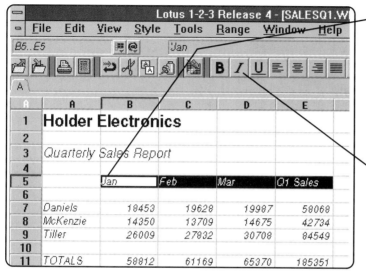

1. **Click** on Jan in **B5**. Leave the pointer in the cell.

2. **Press and hold** the mouse button and **drag** the pointer over to Q1 Sales in E5. Then release the mouse button.

3. **Click** on the **Italics SmartIcon** (the large, slanted I). The text in all the cells will be italicized.

UNDERLINING TEXT

If you have been following along with these examples, cells B5 to E5 are highlighted.

1. **Click** on the **Underline SmartIcon** (the large, underlined U). The highlighted text from the previous section will be underlined.

2. **Click anywhere** on the worksheet to remove the highlighting so you can see the italics and underlining in cells B5 to E5.

Lotus 1-2-3 Release 4 - [SALESQ1.W

File   Edit   View   Style   Tools   Range   Window   Help

B5..E5   Jan

	A	B	C	D	E
1	Holder Electronics				
2					
3	Quarterly Sales Report				
4					
5		Jan	Feb	Mar	Q1 Sales
6					
7	Daniels	18453	19628	19987	58068
8	McKenzie	14350	13709	14675	42734
9	Tiller	26009	27832	30708	84549
10					
11	TOTALS	58812	61169	65370	185351

CREATING A DOUBLE UNDERLINE

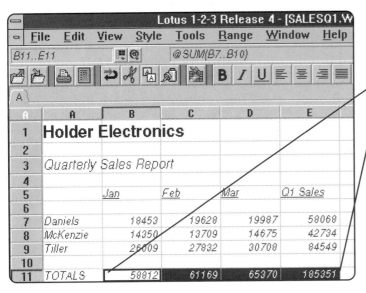

In this section, you will put a double underline beneath the totals in row 11.

1. Click on **B11**. Leave the pointer in the cell.

2. Press and hold the mouse button and **drag** the pointer over to **E11**.

3. Release the mouse button when you have highlighted B11 through E11.

4. Click on **Style** in the menu bar. A pull-down menu will appear.

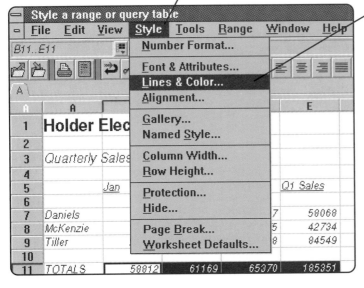

5. Click on **Lines & Color**. The Lines & Color dialog box will appear.

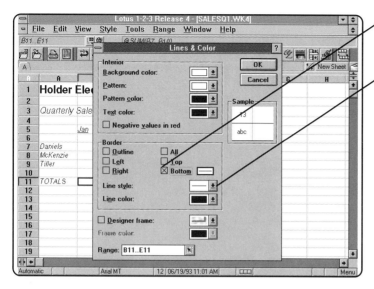

6. Click on **Bottom** to insert an × in the box.

7. Click on ⬇ to the right of the line box. A drop-down list of underline options will appear.

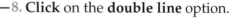

8. Click on the **double line** option.

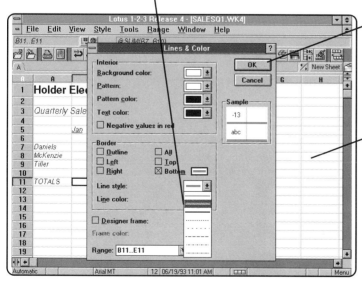

9. Click on **OK**. The Lines & Color dialog box will close and the highlighted cells will have a bottom border of a double underline.

10. Click anywhere on the worksheet to remove the highlighting so you can see the double underline.

Notice that the double underline border is applied to the cell itself. This contrasts with the underline feature in the previous section, which applied to the *contents* of the cell.

CENTERING ACROSS COLUMNS AND WITHIN CELLS

Text is normally aligned on the left in a cell. In this section, you will highlight rows 1 through 5 and apply the centering option to all of them at the same time.

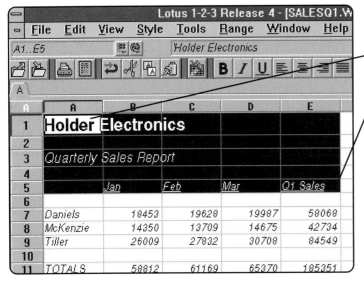

1. Click on **A1**. Leave the pointer in the cell.

2. Press and hold the mouse button and **drag** the pointer diagonally down to **E5**.

3. Release the mouse button when you have highlighted cells A1 to E5.

4. Click on **Style** in the menu bar. A pull-down menu will appear.

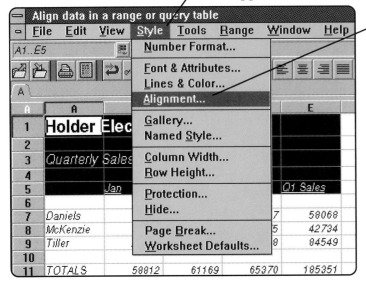

5. Click on **Alignment**. The Alignment dialog box will appear.

6. **Click** on **Center** to insert a dot in the circle.

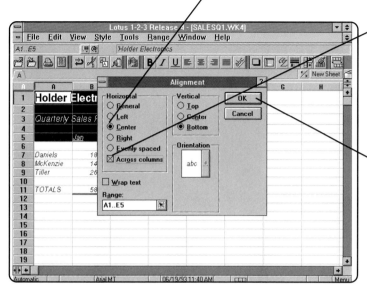

7. **Click** on **Across columns** to insert an ✕ in the box. This will center the company name and worksheet title across the highlighted columns.

8. **Click** on **OK**.

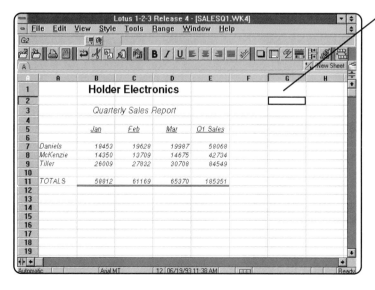

9. **Click anywhere** on the worksheet to remove the highlighting and see the centering.

You will format the numbers on the worksheet in the next chapter.

Formatting Numbers and Working with Styles

The standard format for numbers is called the Automatic number format. You can change this format so that numbers appear with dollar signs, commas, decimals, or percentages; rounded off to a specific decimal place or whole number; or with a minus sign or parentheses to indicate a negative number. You can format numbers to appear as dates or times, or in a specialized format called scientific notation.

You can even save specific formatting as a style, and then apply that style to another set of numbers with a mouse click. The status bar will give you information about the formatting in a specific cell. In this chapter, you will do the following:

❖ Format the numbers already in a worksheet
❖ Format non-adjacent cells with a single command
❖ Save a specific format as a style and apply that style to other numbers
❖ Remove and restore styles in a worksheet
❖ Learn to read the status bar

INSERTING COMMAS IN NUMBERS

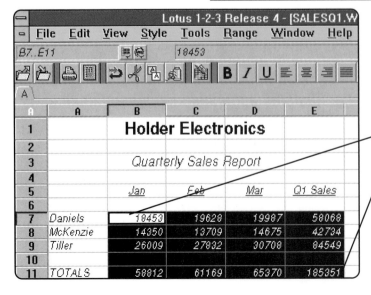

A worksheet can be set up in advance for a specific format. You can also format numbers after you enter them.

1. **Click** on **B7**. Leave the pointer in the cell.

2. **Press and hold** the mouse button and **drag** the pointer diagonally down to E11.

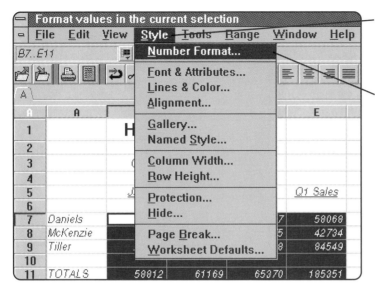

3. **Click** on **Style** in the menu bar. A pull-down menu will appear.

4. **Click** on **Number Format.** The Number Format dialog box will appear.

5. **Click** on **Comma**. A Decimal places box will appear to the right of the Format box with the number 2. This means that numbers will be reformatted to appear with two decimal places even though you didn't enter them that way. Notice the Sample box in the lower right corner of the dialog box. This box shows how a number will look in the highlighted format. You can remove the decimal places.

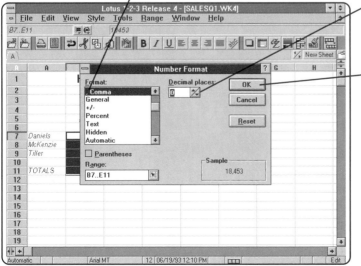

6. **Click** on the **down arrow** in the Decimal places box to set the decimal places to 0.

7. **Click** on **OK**. The dialog box will disappear and the numbers will be formatted with a comma and no decimal places.

This formatting applies only to the highlighted range. A number entered outside this range will appear in the Automatic format.

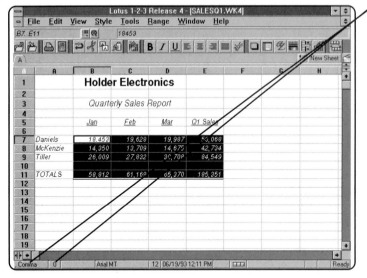

Notice the formatting of the numbers shown in the status bar at the bottom of the worksheet. You can change number formatting in the status bar. You will do this in the next example.

ADDING DOLLAR SIGNS

In this section, you will add dollar signs to the first and last rows of numbers with one command. Normally, you cannot highlight non-adjacent rows. However, if you use the Ctrl key, you can highlight non-adjacent rows (or columns, or cells) and apply a command to all highlighted areas at once.

1. Click on **B7**. Leave the pointer in the cell.

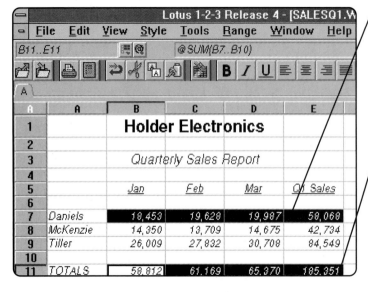

2. Press and **hold** the mouse button and **drag** the pointer over to **E7**.

3. Release the mouse button when you have highlighted the range B7:E7. (B7:E7 is another way to say B7 to E7.)

4. Press and hold the **Ctrl** key and **repeat steps 1 through 3** to **highlight cells B11 to F11**. When you use the Ctrl key, you can select non-adjacent cells or ranges.

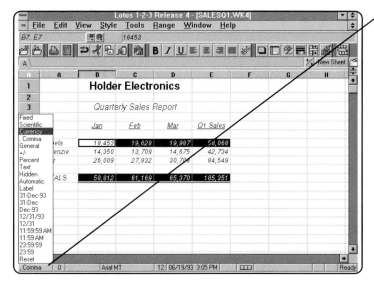

5. Click on **Comma** in the status bar. A pop-up list will appear.

6. Click on **Currency**. The highlighted lines will be formatted with dollar signs.

Note: A number that has been reformatted with dollar signs and decimal places may become too large for the cell. It will appear as ***. See the section "Increasing Column Width" in Chapter 12 to widen the column.

NAMING A STYLE

Number format, font, borders, and alignment are some of the elements that make up the "style" of a cell. If you use a certain style frequently, you don't have to re-create it every time you use it. You can save it as a Named Style and then apply the Named Style to another cell or range. In this section you will select cell B11 and name the style of the cell "totals."

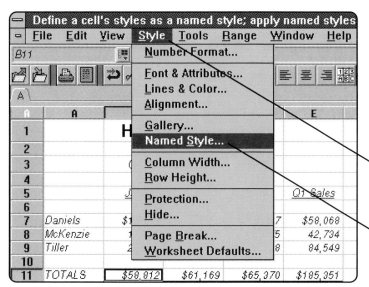

1. Click on **B11**.

2. Click on **Style** in the menu bar. A pull-down menu will appear.

3. Click on **Named Style**. The Named Style dialog box will appear.

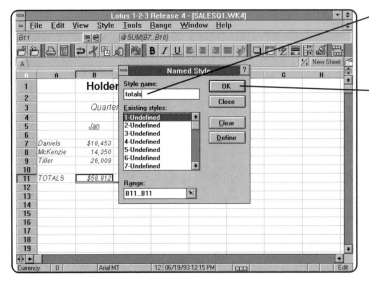

4. Because the cursor is flashing in the style name box, simply **type totals**.

5. Click on **OK**. The dialog box will close. You have now created a style, named totals, that includes a double underline border at the bottom of the cell and a number formatted as currency with no decimal places.

REMOVING AND RESTORING FORMATS AND STYLES

If you decide you don't like a particular format or style, you can remove it with the Undo command on the Edit pull-down menu if you use it immediately after applying the style. There are, however, other ways to remove unwanted styles.

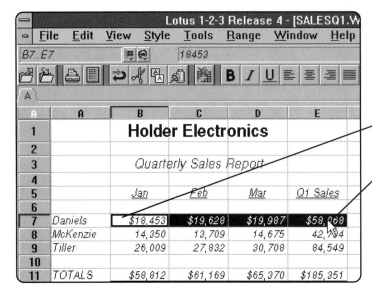

Removing a Format with a Shortcut Menu

1. Click on **B7** and leave the pointer in the cell.

2. Press and hold the mouse button and **drag** the highlight bar across to **E7**. Leave the arrow in E7.

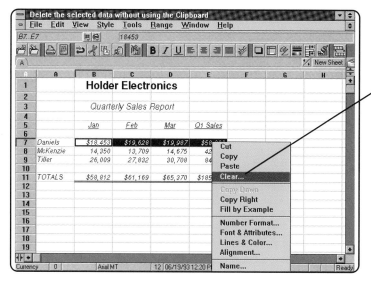

3. **Click** the **right** mouse button. A quick menu will appear.

4. **Click** on **Clear**. The Clear dialog box will appear.

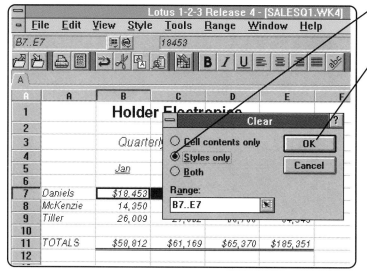

5. **Click** on **Styles only** to insert a dot in the circle.

6. **Click** on **OK**. The dialog box will close and the formatting styles you applied to the highlighted cells will be removed.

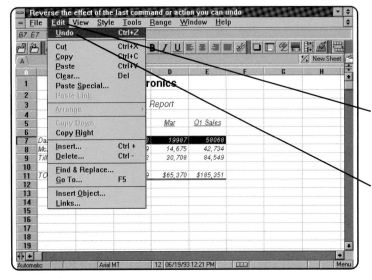

Restoring the Deleted Formatting

1. Click on **Edit** in the menu bar. A pull-down menu will appear.

2. Click on **Undo**. The formatting will be restored. (You can also click on the Undo SmartIcon instead of doing steps 1 and 2.)

Removing a Style with a SmartIcon

If you do not have the Formatting SmartIcon set on your screen, see the section "Changing the SmartIcons" at the beginning of Chapter 9.

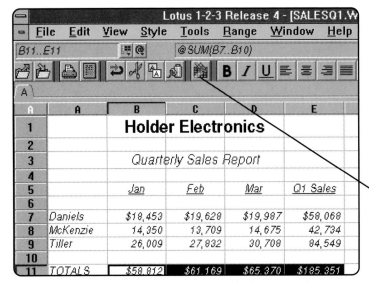

1. Click on **B11** and leave the pointer in the cell.

2. Press and hold the mouse button and **drag** the highlighting over to **E11**. Then release the mouse button.

3. Click on the **Remove Styles SmartIcon.** Any styles you applied to the highlighted cells will be removed.

Using the Status Bar to Apply a Named Style

First, highlight the cell or range to which you want to apply a Named Style. If you have been following along with these examples, B11:E11 is already highlighted.

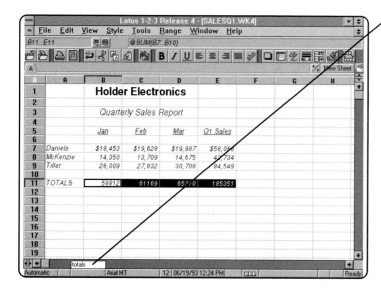

1. Click on the **Named Styles button** in the status bar. It is located to the left of Arial MT. (The button face is blank because the highlighted cells do not have a named style.) A pop-up list of named styles will appear. Because you have named only one style so far, there will be only one style on the list.

2. Click on **totals**. The "totals" style you created earlier in this chapter will be applied to the highlighted cells, and "totals" will appear on the button face in the status bar.

3. Click on the **Save SmartIcon** to save your work.

READING THE STATUS BAR

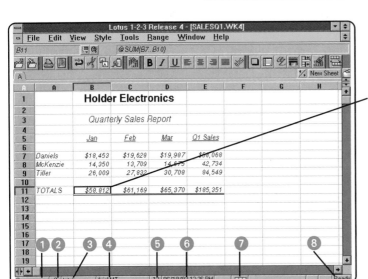

The status bar gives you useful information about a cell.

1. Click on **B11.**

The status bar at the bottom of the worksheet contains the following information:

➊ **Currency** = The number formatting in this cell.

➋ **0** = The number of decimal places in this cell.

➌ **totals** = The Named Style in this cell.

➍ **Arial MT** = The font.

➎ **12** = The size of the font.

➏ **Date/Time**. Click on the button to show cell height and width. Click again to change it back to Date/Time.

➐ Click to show a list of SmartIcon sets. The set currently on your screen will be highlighted.

➑ **Ready** = The mode in which you perform basic functions. Other modes are Edit (for editing) and Value (for writing formulas).

These buttons display information appropriate to the selected cell. If the selected cell does not have a named style, for example, the Named Style button will be blank.

SWITCHING TO THE DEFAULT SmartIcons

In this section, you will switch back to the default tool bar.

1. **Click** on the **SmartIcon button** in the status bar. A pop-up list of SmartIcon sets will appear.

2. **Click** on **Default**. The standard set of SmartIcons will replace the Formatting SmartIcons.

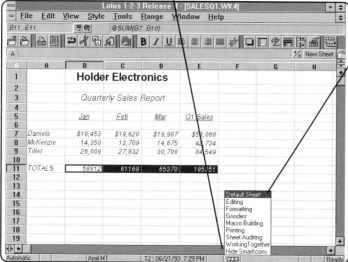

3. **Click** on the **Save SmartIcon** to save your work.

Program Manager

Part III: Multiple Worksheets and Formulas

Adding Work-
sheets to a File

You can add worksheets to a file and create a multiple-sheet file. You can have up to 256 worksheets in a single file. Tabs allow you to switch back and forth between worksheets. You can copy information from one worksheet to another. In this chapter, you will do the following:

❖ Add a second worksheet to a file

❖ Switch back and forth between two worksheets

❖ Copy data from one worksheet and paste it into a second worksheet

❖ Place names on worksheet tabs

❖ Delete a worksheet

ADDING A
SECOND WORKSHEET

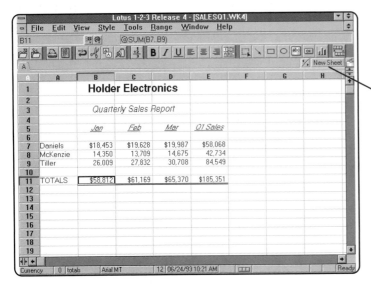

1. **Open** the **SALESQ1** worksheet if it is not already on your screen.

2. **Click** on the **New Sheet button**. A new worksheet will appear.

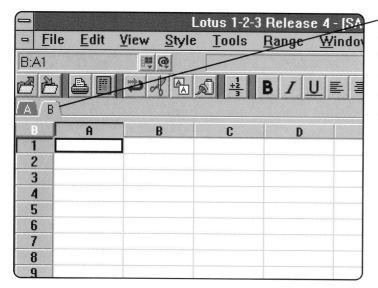

Notice that the new worksheet tab is labeled B. Tab B is the lighter-colored tab because worksheet B is the *current* (active) worksheet.

SWITCHING BETWEEN WORKSHEETS

In this section, you will move back and forth between SALESQ1 and worksheet B.

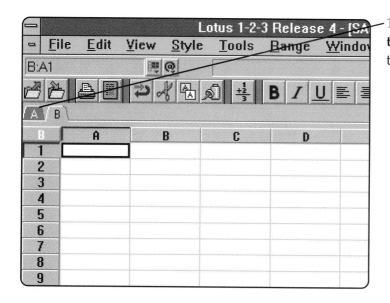

1. **Click** on the **worksheet A tab**. SALESQ1 will come to the foreground.

COPYING BETWEEN WORKSHEETS

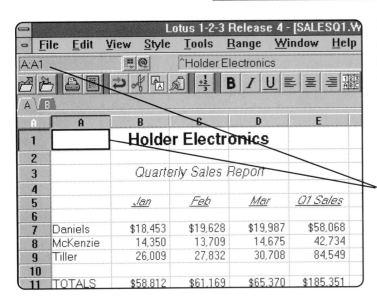

In this example, you will copy the heading from SALESQ1 to worksheet B using a quick menu.

Using a Quick Menu

1. Click on **A1** in SALESQ1. Leave the pointer in the cell. Notice the cell indicator says that this cell is A:A1. This shows that it is cell A1 on worksheet A.

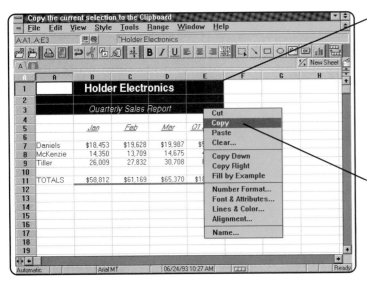

2. Press and hold the mouse button and **drag** the highlight bar to **E3**. *Leave the pointer in the highlighted area.*

3. Click the *right* mouse button. A quick menu will appear.

4. Click on **Copy**. The quick menu will disappear. There will be no other difference in your screen, but the highlighted cells are now copied to the *Clipboard*, a storage area that holds copied, deleted, or cleared data. The data will stay in the Clipboard until it is replaced with other data.

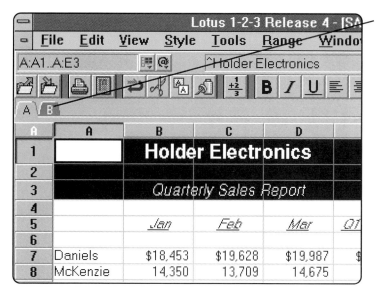

5. Click on the **worksheet B tab** to bring the new worksheet to the foreground.

6. Click on cell **B:A1** if it is not already selected. *Leave the mouse pointer in the cell.*

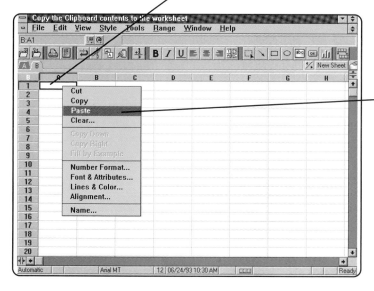

7. Click the *right* mouse button. A quick menu will appear.

8. Click on **Paste**. The copied cells will appear on worksheet B beginning at cell A1.

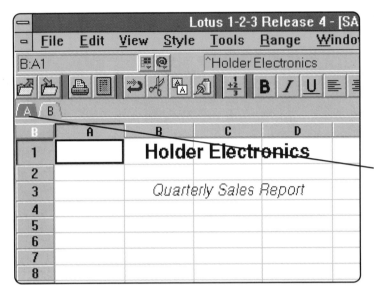

Worksheet B will look like this example.

This heading is not exactly right for this worksheet. You will edit it in the next chapter.

9. **Click** on the **A tab** to move back to Worksheet A.

Using the Copy and Paste SmartIcons

In this example, you will copy the salespeople's names from Worksheet A and paste them into Worksheet B.

1. **Click** on Daniels in **A7**. *Leave the pointer in the cell.*

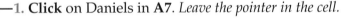

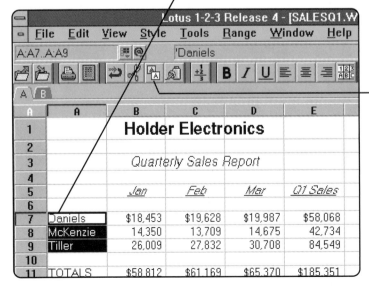

2. **Press and hold** the mouse button and **drag** the cursor down to Tiller in **A9**.

3. **Click** on the **Copy SmartIcon**. You won't see any difference in your screen, but the highlighted cells are now copied to the Clipboard.

4. **Click** on the **Worksheet B tab** to move to the second worksheet.

5. **Click** on cell **B5**. *Leave the pointer in the cell.*

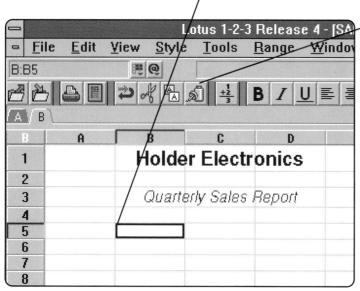

6. **Click** on the **Paste SmartIcon**. The copied text will be pasted into this worksheet beginning at B5.

You will move these names to other cells in the next chapter.

NAMING WORKSHEETS

You can put a worksheet name on each tab so that it's easier to remember what each worksheet is about.

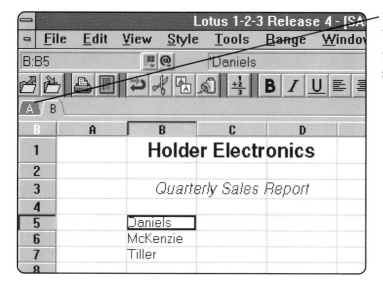

1. **Click twice** on the **A tab**. Worksheet A will move to the foreground and the tab space will get wider.

2. **Type SalesQ1** (with no spaces) and **press Enter**.

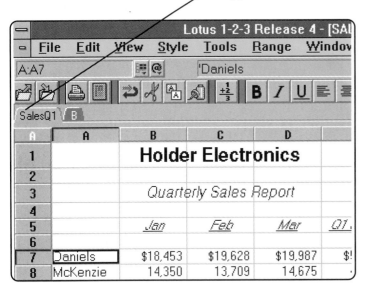

There are a number of rules about worksheet names. Among these are:

❖ Worksheet names can be up to 15 characters long.

❖ Don't use spaces. Use an underline to separate words.

❖ Don't create worksheet names that look like cell addresses, such as Q1 for Quarter 1.

Refer to the **User's Guide** for additional rules.

3. **Click twice** on the **B tab**. Worksheet B will move to the foreground and the tab will get wider.

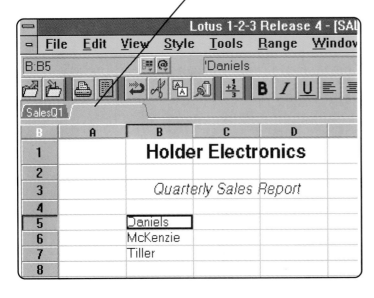

4. **Type JanComm** (for January Commissions). **Press Enter**.

DELETING A WORKSHEET

In this example, you will add another worksheet to the file, and then delete it.

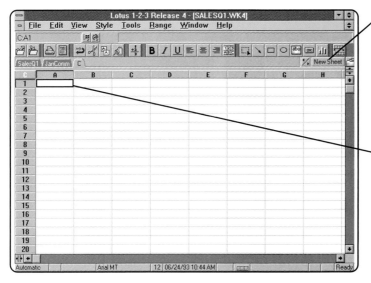

1. Click on **New Sheet**. Worksheet C will appear on your screen.

To delete a worksheet, click on any cell in the worksheet.

2. Click on cell **A1** if it is not already selected.

3. Click on **Edit** in the menu bar. A pull-down menu will appear.

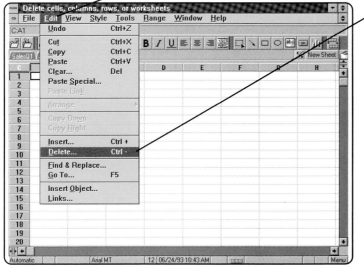

4. Click on **Delete**. The Delete dialog box will appear.

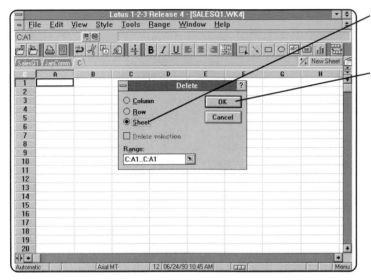

5. Click on **Sheet** to insert a dot in the circle.

6. Click on **OK**. Sheet C will disappear.

7. Click on the **Save SmartIcon** to save your work.

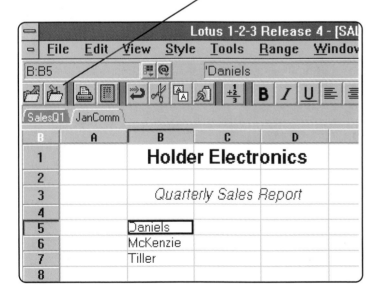

You will format the JanComm worksheet in the next chapter, "Formatting a Second Worksheet."

Formatting a Second Worksheet

In addition to the standard Windows functions of copying and pasting, 1-2-3 has a new feature, called drag-and-drop moving, that will come in handy as you format the second worksheet. In this chapter, you will do the following:

❖ Move data on a worksheet with drag-and-drop moving

❖ Pre-format the worksheet so that all numbers appear in a specific format

❖ Use the Copy Right feature to copy data to adjacent cells

DRAG-AND-DROP MOVING

If you followed the steps in Chapter 11, you copied the heading and the salespeople's names from the SalesQ1 worksheet to the JanComm worksheet in the SALESQ1.WK4 file. If not, you will need to follow the steps in Chapter 11 before you do these procedures.

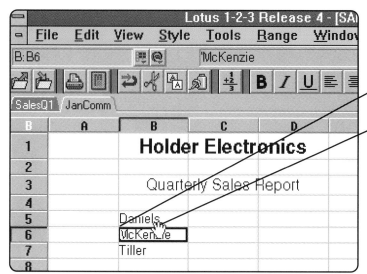

In this section, you will move McKenzie and Tiller up to row 5.

1. **Click** on McKenzie in **B6**.

2. **Move** the pointer to the **top border** of the cell. The pointer will change to an open hand. You may have to fiddle with the placement of the pointer to get it to change.

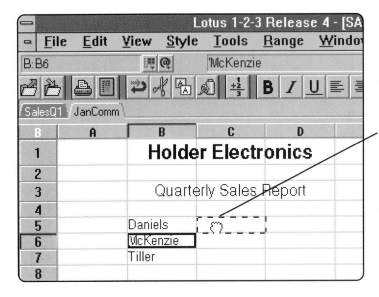

3. Press and hold the mouse button and **drag** the cell by its border up to **C5**. You will see a closed hand dragging the cell.

4. Release the mouse button when the outline is in C5. The contents of the cell will move to C5. (Isn't this cool?!)

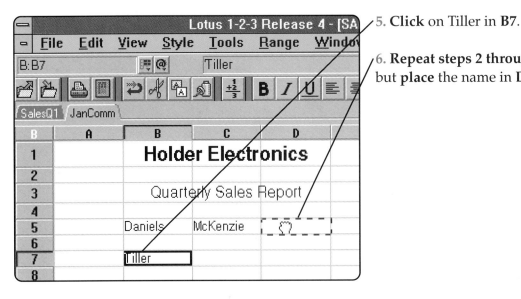

5. **Click** on Tiller in **B7**.

6. **Repeat steps 2 through 4**, but **place** the name in **D5**.

PRE-FORMATTING NUMBERS

In this section, you will set up the worksheet for a specific number format. Any number entered into the worksheet will appear in the specified format.

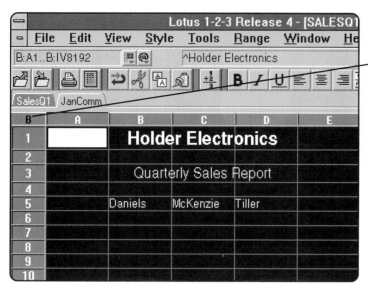

1. **Click** on the **worksheet selection button** at the intersection of the row numbers and column headings. The entire worksheet will be highlighted in black (with the exception of the first cell in the range, which will remain white).

2. **Click** on **Style** in the menu bar. A pull-down menu will appear.

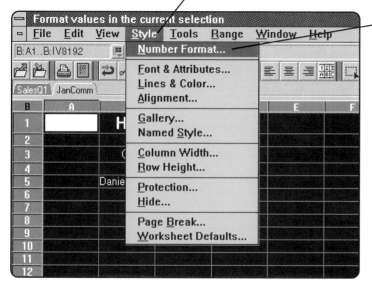

3. **Click** on **Number Format**. The Number Format dialog box will appear.

4. Click on **,Comma.** The Decimal places box will appear to the right.

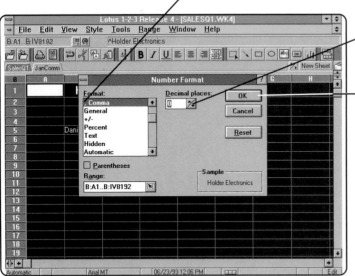

5. Click twice on ▼ to change Decimal places to **0.**

6. Click on **OK.** The Number Format dialog box will disappear.

7. Click anywhere on the worksheet to remove the highlighting.

EDITING COPIED DATA

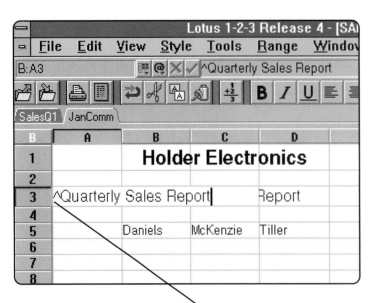

In this section, you will change the report name to "January Commission Report."

1. Click on **B3.** Nothing appears in the contents box. How strange! As far as 1-2-3 is concerned, "Quarterly Sales Report" is in A3 where you originally entered it. The fact that you centered it across columns affects only its appearance, not its original placement.

2. Click twice on **A3** to open the cell for in-cell editing. "Quarterly Sales Report" will appear in the cell. It's okay that "Report" still seems to be in D3.

3. **Place** the cursor at the **beginning** of the **cell**. It will change to an I-beam.

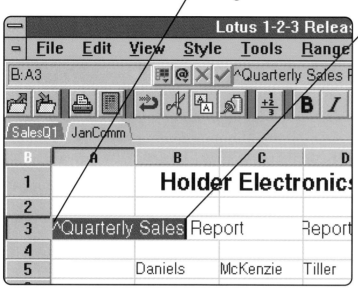

4. **Press and hold** the mouse button and **drag** the highlight bar over **Quarterly Sales**. Make sure you don't highlight the space after "Sales" or you will delete the space between the words when you make the correction.

5. **Type January Commission**. It will replace the highlighted text.

6. **Click** on ✔ (or press Enter) to enter the change in the cell.

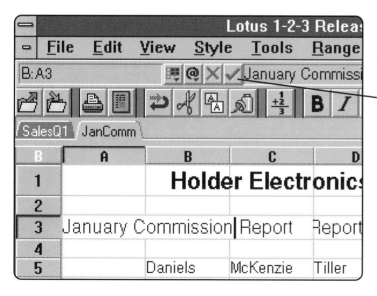

INCREASING COLUMN WIDTH

You can increase column width with a menu command or with the mouse. Use a menu command when you want to increase a column to a specific width.

Using a Menu Command

In this section, you will add the salespeople's first names to the worksheet. The longest name will have 15 characters. Therefore, you can increase the width of columns B, C, and D to 15 using a menu command.

1. **Click** on Daniels in **B5**. *Leave the pointer in the cell.*

2. **Press and hold** the mouse button and **drag** the pointer over to Tiller in **D5**. The three names will be highlighted.

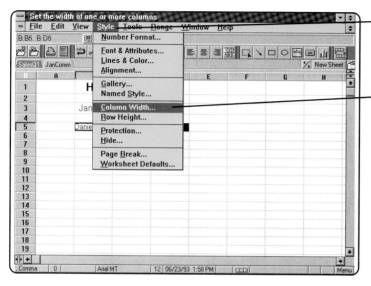

3. **Click** on **Style** in the menu bar. A pull-down menu will appear.

4. **Click** on **Column Width**. The Column Width dialog box will appear.

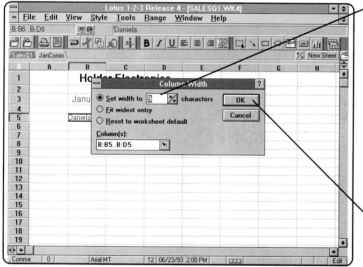

Notice that 9 in the Column Width box is highlighted. This is the standard (default) column width in 1-2-3.

5. **Type 15** to increase the column width of the selected columns to 15. The 15 will replace the highlighted number 9.

6. **Click** on **OK**. Columns B, C, and D will be 15 characters wide.

Notice that the headings in rows 1 and 3 centered themselves over the wider columns.

7. Click twice on Daniels in **B5** to open the cell for in-cell editing. The cursor will be flashing at the end of Daniels.

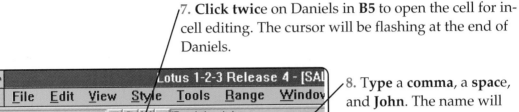

8. Type a **comma**, a **space**, and **John**. The name will become Daniels, John.

9. Press Enter.

10. Repeat steps 7 through 9 to change McKenzie in C5 to **McKenzie, Susan**.

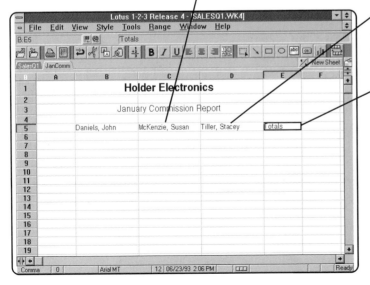

11. Repeat steps 7 through 9 to change Tiller in D5 to **Tiller, Stacey**.

12. Click on E5. On your screen it will be empty.

13. Type Totals.

14. Press Enter.

Using the Mouse

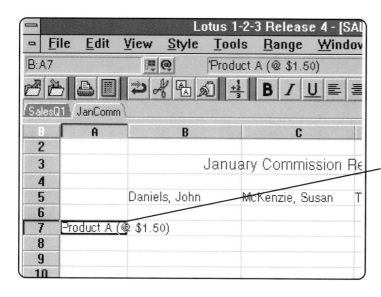

In this section, you will use the mouse to increase the width of column A. When you use the mouse, 1-2-3 adjusts the column for the longest entry, called a *best fit* adjustment.

1. **Click** on **A7**.

2. **Type Product A (@ $1.50)**.

3. **Press Enter** to insert the phrase in **A7**. Notice that the entry is too wide for the cell.

4. **Move** the mouse pointer up to the column headings. Place it on **the line between column A and column B**. It will change shape as shown in the example when you get it positioned correctly.

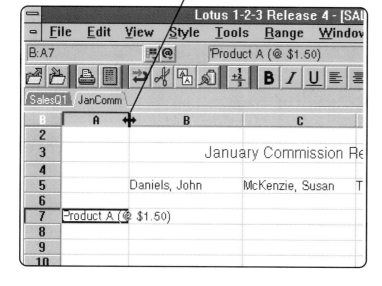

5. **Click twice** on the left mouse button. The column will increase to a best fit width.

Notice that the headings in rows 1 and 3 centered themselves again to accommodate the wider column A.

ENTERING ROW HEADINGS

1. **Click** on **A8**. On your screen, it will be empty.

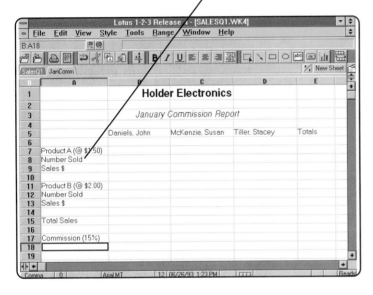

2. **Type Number Sold**.

3. **Press** the ↓ key to insert the words into A8 and move to A9. (If you are using the arrow keys on on the numeric keypad, make sure Num Lock and Scroll Lock are turned off.

4. **Type** the **row headings** listed below in the appropriate cells:

A9   Sales $

A10

A11   Product B (@ $2.00)

A12*   Number Sold

A13*   Sales $

A14

A15   Total Sales

A16

A17   Commission (15%)

* You can use the Copy and Paste options on the shortcut menu or the SmartIcons to copy Number Sold and Sales $ from A8 and A9 to A12 and A13, respectively. (See the section "Copying Between Worksheets" in Chapter 11 if you need help.)

5. **Click** on the ⬇ to bring row 21 into view.

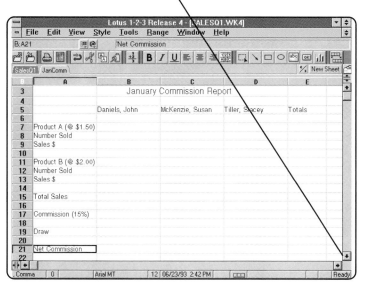

6. **Type** the **row headings** listed below in row 19 and row 21:

A19   Draw

A21   Net Commission

In the next section, you will enter numbers into the worksheet. Then you will write formulas in Chapter 13, "Writing Formulas."

ENTERING NUMBERS

1. **Type** the **numbers** below in the appropriate cells. Because you pre-formatted the numbers to have commas, you don't have to type the commas. They will be inserted by 1-2-3 after you enter the number into the cell. (If you forget and type them, it won't do any harm.)

B8	**C8**	**D8**
3702	4784	5470

B12	**C12**	**D12**
6450	3587	8902

B19
1000

In the next section, you will copy the 1000 in B19 into C19 and D19.

COPYING NUMBERS

You used the Copy Right command in Chapter 4 to copy a formula to several adjacent cells. In this example, you will use Copy Right to copy the contents of a cell.

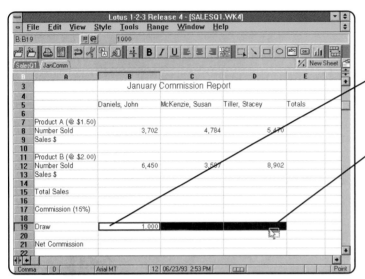

1. **Click** on 1000 in **B19**. Leave the pointer in the cell.

2. **Press and hold** the mouse button and **drag** the pointer over to **D19**. The three cells will be highlighted. *Leave the pointer in* D19.

3. **Click** the **right** mouse button. A quick menu will appear.

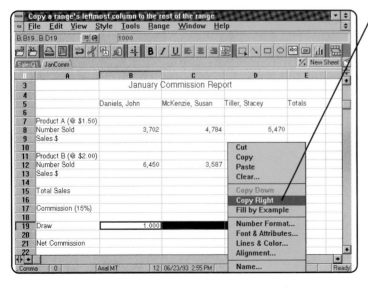

4. **Click** on **Copy Right**. The number 1,000 will be copied to the highlighted cells C19 and D19.

5. **Click anywhere** on your worksheet to remove the highlight.

6. Don't forget to **click** on the **Save SmartIcon** to save all your work.

Writing Formulas

Writing formulas is a breeze in 1-2-3. You use standard symbols for mathematical processes. Addition is symbolized by a plus sign (+); subtraction by a hyphen (-); multiplication by an asterisk (*); and division by a forward slash (/). In this chapter, you will do the following:

❖ Write formulas for addition, subtraction, multiplication, and percentage

❖ Add with the Addition SmartIcon

❖ Copy formulas to other cells

WRITING A MULTIPLICATION FORMULA

In this section, you will write a formula to calculate Sales $ = Number Sold x Price.

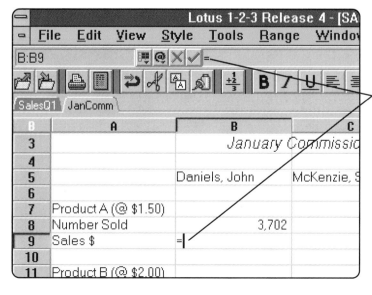

1. **Click** on **B9**, the Sales $ cell for Daniels. On your screen, it will be empty.

2. **Type =** to tell 1-2-3 that you are starting a formula. The = will appear in the contents box and in the cell. (You can also use a + to start a formula.)

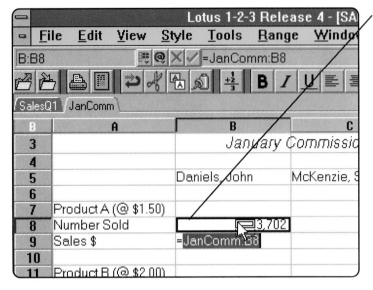

3. Click on 3,702 in **B8** to tell 1-2-3 that this is the first number in the formula. The pointer will have a box with it. The cell address JanComm:B8 will appear in the contents box and in B9.

4. Type * (the symbol for multiplication). The * will appear in the contents box and in B9.

5. Type 1.5 (for $1.50). The number ill appear in the contents box and in B9.

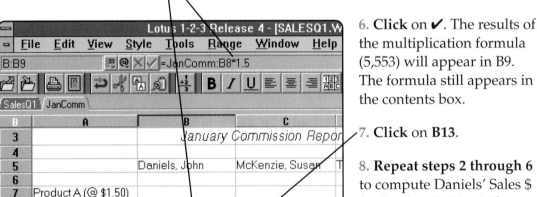

6. Click on ✔. The results of the multiplication formula (5,553) will appear in B9. The formula still appears in the contents box.

7. Click on **B13**.

8. Repeat steps 2 through 6 to compute Daniels' Sales $ for Product B. Use 2 (for $2.00) as the price. The formula is B13=JanComm:B12*2. You will see 12,900 in B13 when you finish.

WRITING AN ADDITION FORMULA

In this section you will write a formula to calculate Total Sales:

(Total Sales = Sales $ for Product A + Sales $ for Product B)

1. **Click** on **B15**, the Total Sales cell for Daniels. On your screen, it will be empty.

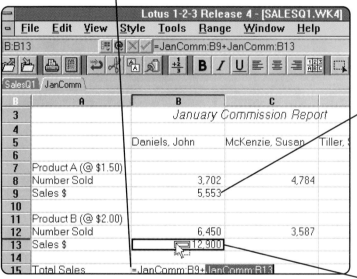

2. **Type =** to indicate the start of a formula. The = will appear in the cell and in the contents box.

3. **Click** on 5,553 in **B9**. The cell address (JanComm:B9) will appear in B15 and in the contents box.

4. **Type +** to indicate addition. The + will appear in the contents box and in B15

5. **Click** on 12,900 in **B13**. The cell address will appear in the contents box and in B15.

6. **Click** on ✔. Lotus 1-2-3 will make the calculations and enter the result of the formula (18,453) into B15.

WRITING A FORMULA TO CALCULATE A PERCENT

In this section, you will write a formula to calculate Commission = Total Sales x 15 percent.

1. **Click** on **B17**, the Commission cell for Daniels. On your screen it will be empty.

2. **Type =** to tell 1-2-3 that you are starting a formula.

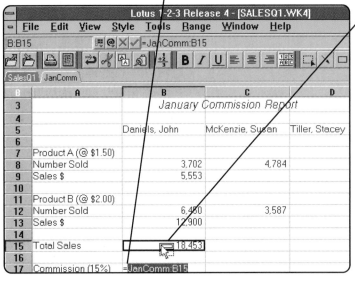

3. **Click** on 18,453 in **B15**. The cell address will appear in the contents box and in B17.

4. **Type *** to indicate multiplication. The * will appear in the contents box and in B17.

5. **Type 15%** to multiply 18,453 by 15 percent. It will appear in the contents box and in B17.

6. **Click** on ✔ or press Enter. Lotus will make the calculations and enter the result (2,768) into B17. Fifteen percent of 18,453 is actually 2,767.95. Because you selected a number format with no decimal places, the number will be rounded to the nearest whole number.

WRITING A SUBTRACTION FORMULA

In this section, you will write a formula to calculate Net Commission = Commission - Draw.

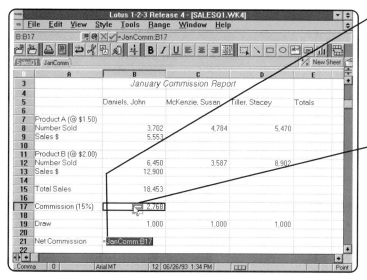

1. Click on **B21**. On your screen it will be empty.

2. Type = to start a formula. The = will appear in the contents box and in B21.

3. Click on **B17**. The cell address (JanComm:B17) will appear in the contents box and in B21.

4. Type - to indicate subtraction.

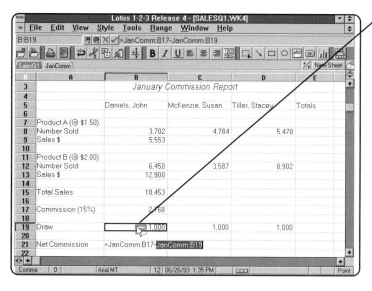

5. Click on **B19**. The cell address will be added to the contents box and to B21.

6. Click on **✔**. Lotus will make the calculations and enter the result (1,768) into B21.

MORE ABOUT FORMULAS

Formulas in 1-2-3 can be as simple or complex as you like. However, most will contain the basic arithmetic operations of addition, subtraction, multiplication, and division.

If you include more than one operation in a formula, 1-2-3 performs them in the order shown to the left.

For example, in the formula 10-2*3, the * is performed first, giving a product of 6. Then the subtraction is performed, giving a final answer of 4.

Putting parentheses in a formula will cause 1-2-3 to perform the calculation within the parentheses before all others. When a set of parentheses is inside another set of parentheses, the calculation of the inside parentheses is performed first, and then the calculation required by the outside parentheses. Within parentheses, the precedence order above applies. Look at the order in which the functions are performed in the following example:

Arithmetic operations are performed in the following order:
1. * Multiplication
2. / Division
3. + Addition
4. - Subtraction

$$325 + ((500 + B7) * 4) / 8 - E25$$

| | | | | |
| 4th | 1st | 2nd | 3rd | 5th |

Consult the *User's Guide* that came with your documentation for a thorough discussion of formulas.

ADDING WITH THE ADDITION SmartIcon

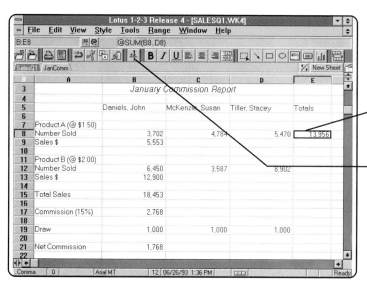

In this section, you will use the Addition SmartIcon to add the figures in rows 8, 12, and 19.

1. **Click** on **E8**. On your screen, it will be empty.

2. **Click** on the **Addition SmartIcon**. The sum of row 8 (13,956) will appear in E8.

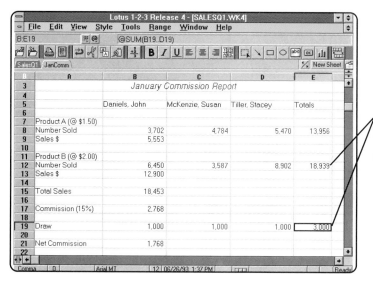

3. **Repeats steps 1 through 2** to enter the totals into E12 (18,939) and E19 (3,000).

COPYING FORMULAS

Now that all your formulas are written, you can copy them to other cells.

1. **Click** on **B9**. Leave the pointer in the cell. (If the formula mysteriously appears instead of the cell pointer, simply press Enter to see the number and the cell pointer.

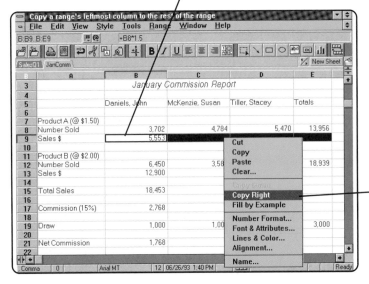

2. **Press and hold** the mouse button and **drag** the highlight bar over to **E9**. *Leave the pointer in the last cell.*

3. **Click** the *right* mouse button. A quick menu will appear.

4. **Click** on **Copy Right**. The addition formula will be copied and the totals will be inserted into the highlighted cells.

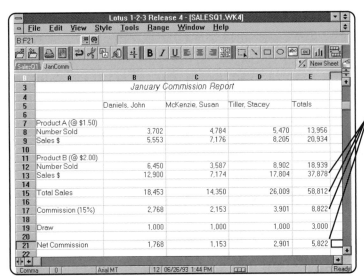

5. **Repeat steps 1 to 4** to copy the formulas in rows 13, 15, 17, and 21. Your worksheet will look like the example to the left.

6. Don't forget to **save**.

Using the Style Gallery

The Style Gallery is another of 1-2-3's special features. It contains a selection of pre-designed formats that you can apply to your worksheet. You can even modify the pre-designed style. In this chapter, you will do the following:

❖ Select a style from the Style Gallery

❖ Remove a style from a worksheet

❖ Modify the pre-designed style

SELECTING A STYLE FROM THE STYLE GALLERY

In this section, you will choose a style from the Style Gallery and apply it to the JanComm worksheet. In this example, you will not change the style of the heading; therefore, you will not include it in the range of cells to be styled.

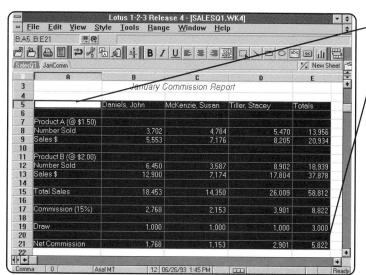

1. Click on **A5**. Leave the pointer in the cell.

2. Press and hold the mouse button and **drag** the highlight bar **over to E5** and **down to row 21**. Then release the mouse button.

3. **Click** on **Style** in the menu bar. A pull-down menu will appear.

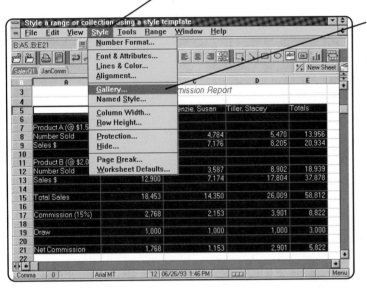

4. **Click** on **Gallery**. The Gallery dialog box will appear.

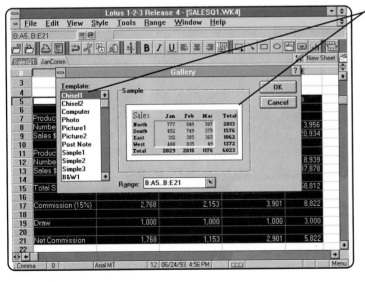

Notice that the sample worksheet appears in the highlighted style. In this example, the Sample shown is Chisel1.

5. **Click** on **Chisel2** and notice the sample worksheet change.

6. **Click** on **each of the options** in the list to see what each looks like.

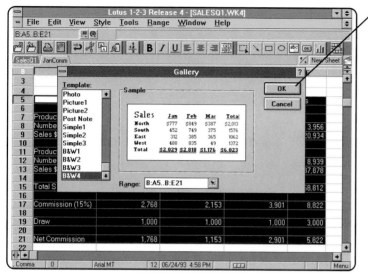

7. When you have highlighted the last choice on the list, B&W4, **click** on **OK**. The dialog box will close and your worksheet will be formatted in this style8.

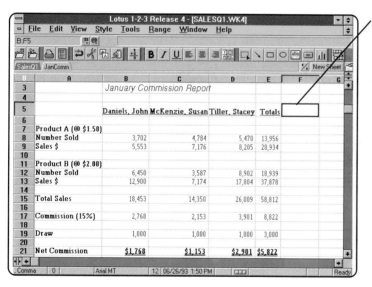

8. Click on **any empty cell** to remove the highlighting from the worksheet so you can see the applied style.

REMOVING A GALLERY STYLE

In this section, you will remove the B&W4 style from the worksheet.

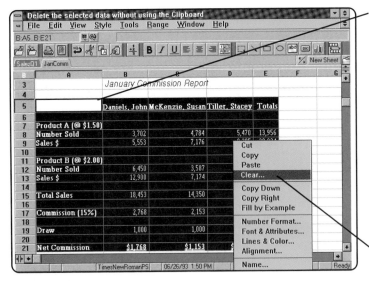

1. **Click** on **A5**. Leave the cursor in the cell.

2. **Press and hold** the mouse button and **drag** the highlight bar down to **E21**. *Leave the pointer in the highlighted area.*

3. **Click** the *right* mouse button. A quick menu will appear.

4. **Click** on **Clear**. The Clear dialog box will appear.

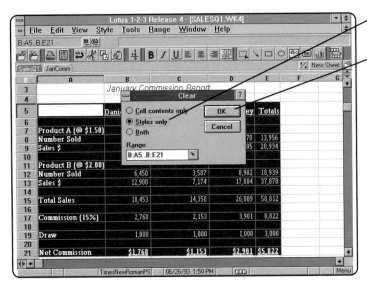

5. **Click** on **Styles only**.

6. **Click** on **OK**. The dialog box will close and the B&W4 style will be removed from the worksheet.

7. **Click** on **any empty cell** to remove the highlighting from the worksheet.

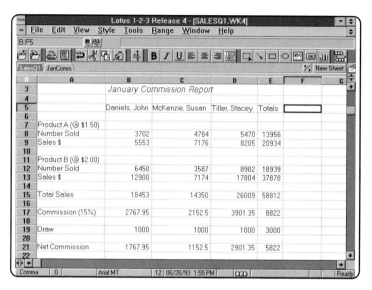

Notice that *all styles* were removed from the worksheet so the number formatting you applied to the entire worksheet is gone too.

At this point, you have several options. If you don't like the B&W4 style, you can simply reformat the numbers. Refer to the section "Pre-Formatting Numbers" in Chapter 12 if you need help.

In this example, you will use the Undo SmartIcon to undo the clearing of the styles. You can use the Undo command only if you haven't performed any other function since you cleared the styles.

8. **Click** on the **Undo SmartIcon**. The B&W4 style will reappear on your worksheet.

MODIFYING A GALLERY STYLE

Notice the B&W4 Gallery style changed the column widths you set up for the worksheet. You change a Gallery Style the same way you change any other style. In this example, you will make columns B, C, and D 15 characters wide.

1. **Click** on the **column B heading**. The entire column will be highlighted.

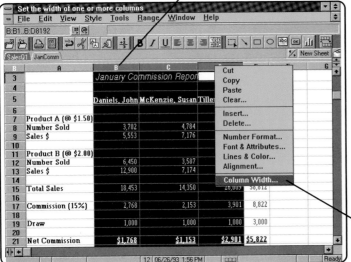

2. **Press and hold** the mouse button and **drag** the pointer across to **column D**. All three columns will be highlighted. *Leave the pointer in the highlighted area.*

3. **Click** the *right* mouse button. A quick menu will appear.

4. **Click** on **Column Width**. The Column Width dialog box will appear.

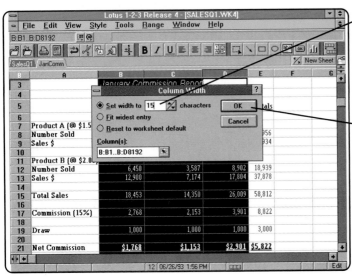
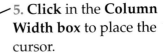

5. **Click** in the **Column Width box** to place the cursor.

6. **Type 15.**

7. **Click** on **OK**. The dialog box will close and the highlighted columns will be changed to 15 characters wide.

Working with Large Worksheets

When you work with a large worksheet, it is annoying to watch the row and column titles scroll out of sight as you move around the worksheet. Lotus solves this problem by letting you freeze the row and column titles on your worksheet so they stay on your screen as you scroll up and down. You can change the view of your worksheet so you can see more on the screen or zoom in to see cells closer up. In this chapter, you will do the following:

❖ Freeze the row and column titles

❖ Change the view of the worksheet to zoom out and in

❖ Change the View Preferences

FREEZING ROW AND COLUMN TITLES

In this section, you will freeze the row and column titles so they are always visible.

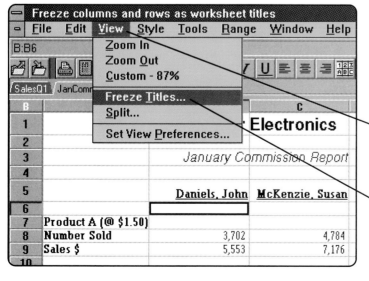

1. **Click** on **B6**. This will be the "freezing point." Rows above this cell will remain in view. Columns to the left of this cell will remain in view.

2. **Click** on **View** in the menu bar. A pull-down menu will appear.

3. **Click** on **Freeze Titles**. The Freeze Titles dialog box will appear.

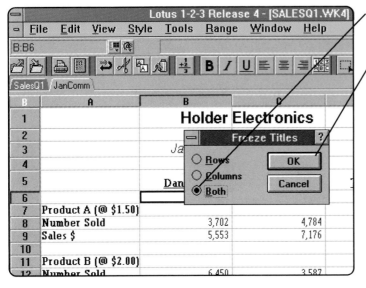

4. Click on **Both** to insert a dot in the circle.

5. Click on **OK**. The dialog box will close and the rows and columns above and to the left of the freezing point will remain on your screen.

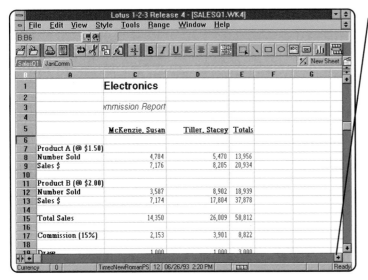

6. Click on ➡ on the bottom scroll bar to scroll to the right.

Notice that the row titles remain on your screen and that column B has scrolled out of sight.

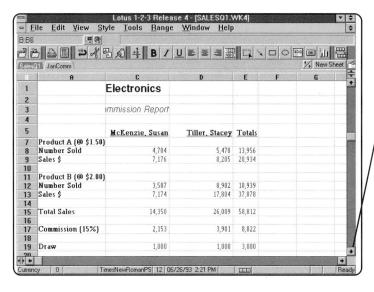

7. Click on ⬇ on the scroll bar at the right to scroll down your screen.

Notice that the column headings remain in view even though row 6 has scrolled out of sight.

Going Home

Normally, when you press the Home key, you return to A1. When you have frozen your worksheet, you will return to the "freezing point," which in this example is B6.

1. Press the **Home** key on your keyboard. You will return to B6.

UNFREEZING TITLES

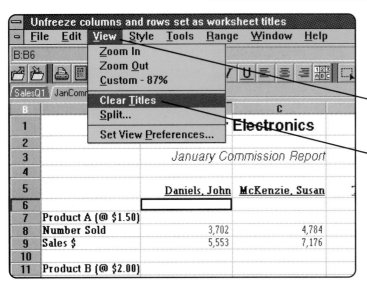

It doesn't matter where the cursor is when you unfreeze titles.

1. Click on **View** in the menu bar.

2. Click on **Clear Titles**.

3. Repeat steps 1 through 3 in "Freezing Row and Column Titles" to "refreeze."

CHANGING THE SCREEN VIEW

The Zoom feature in 1-2-3 is like the zoom lens on a camera. You can *zoom out* and fit more of the worksheet on your screen. Or, you can *zoom in* and magnify a specific area.

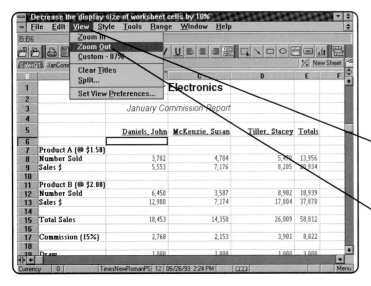

Zooming Out

In this section, you will zoom out so that more of the worksheet is visible on your screen.

1. Click on **View** in the menu bar. A pull-down menu will appear.

2. Click on **Zoom Out.**

3. Repeat steps 1 and 2 to zoom out even more.

Zooming In

1. **Click** on **View** in the menu bar. A pull-down menu will appear.

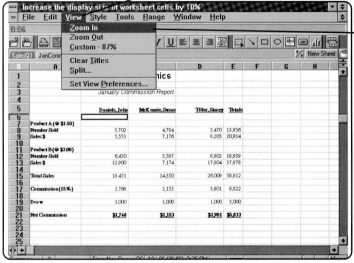

2. **Click** on **Zoom In**.

3. **Repeat steps 1 and 2** to return to the standard view.

If you repeat steps 1 and 2 again, you will magnify a portion of your screen. Experiment a little with different zooms.

SETTING VIEW PREFERENCES

You can customize what you see on your screen, including whether or not you want elements such as the worksheet tabs, grid lines, and page breaks to show. In this example, you will customize the zoom percentage.

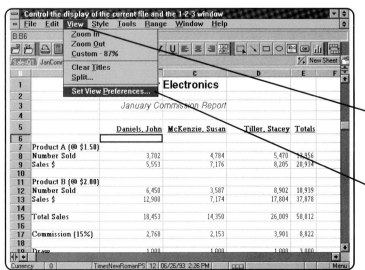

1. **Click** on **View** in the menu bar. A pull-down menu will appear.

2. **Click** on **Set View Preferences**. The Set View Preferences dialog box will appear.

Notice the range of elements you can change on your screen. Click to remove the ✕, and the element will be removed from your screen when you close the dialog box.

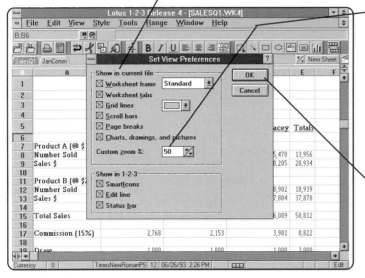

3. Click twice on **87** in the zoom percentage box. It will be highlighted.

4. Type 50. (This is a rather drastic reduction, but it will let you see very clearly how this function operates.)

5. Click on **OK**. The dialog box will close and your worksheet will appear in a 50% zoom.

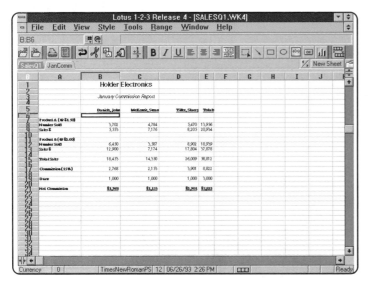

Your worksheet will look like the example to the left.

6. Repeat steps 1 through 5 to change the zoom percentage back to 87 (or whatever percentage you prefer).

Linking Two Files

When you establish a link between two worksheets, any change made in the linked data on the first worksheet (the source, or *server*, worksheet) is immediately reflected in the linked data on the second worksheet (the target, or *client*, worksheet). The process of creating a link is very easy. In this chapter, you will do the following:

❖ Open a new worksheet file

❖ Move back and forth between files

❖ Tile two files on your screen so you can see them both at the same time

❖ Link the files

❖ Test the link

OPENING A NEW FILE

When you open a second worksheet in a file, as you did in the SALESQ1 file, both worksheets are part of the same file. When you save or close one of the worksheets, you save or close the entire file. When you open a new file, however, you are creating an independent worksheet. If you have enough memory, you can have up to 16 independent files on your screen at the same time.

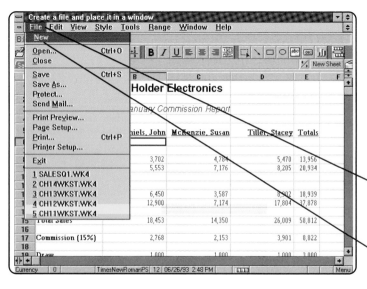

1. Open SALESQ1.WK4 if it is not already on your screen.

2. **Click** on **File** in the menu bar. A pull-down menu will appear.

3. **Click** on **New**. A new worksheet will appear.

Entering Data in the New Worksheet

1. Click on **A**1. On your screen, it will be empty.

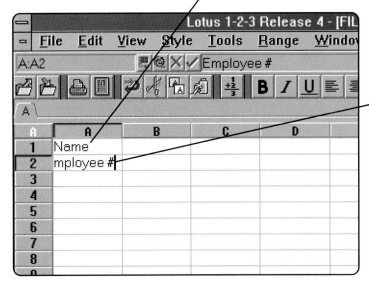

2. Type Name and **press** ↓ on your keyboard to enter the word in the cell and move to A2.

3. Type Employee #. Because the entry is a little too long for the cell, the beginning of the word will scroll out of sight as you type.

4. Press ↓ **twice** to enter "Employee #" in the cell and move down two cells to A4.

Entering a Series of Months

In this section, you will enter a series of months in column A.

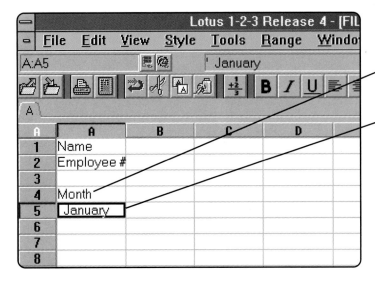

1. Click on **A**4. On your screen, it will be empty.

2. Type Month and **press** ↓ to move down to A5.

3. Press the **spacebar** on your keyboard **twice** and then **type January**. This will indent January two spaces.

4. Press Enter and leave the pointer in the cell.

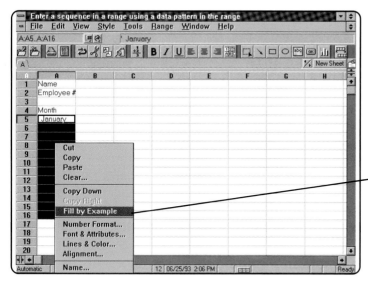

5. **Press and hold** the mouse button and **drag** the pointer down to **A16**. *Leave the pointer in the highlighted area.*

6. **Click** the *right* mouse button. A quick menu will appear.

7. **Click** on **Fill by Example**. The series January through December will appear. Notice the entire series is indented two spaces.

Increasing Cell Width

In this section, you will use the mouse to increase the width of column A.

1. **Move** the mouse pointer up to the column headings and **place** it on the **line between columns A and B**. The pointer will change shape.

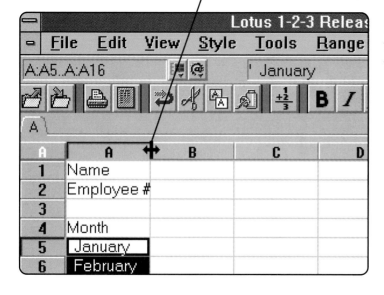

2. **Click twice**. The column will expand to a best fit width.

Entering a Number as Text

In this section, you will enter an employee's name and employment number. Because the employment number is for identification purposes only, you don't want 1-2-3 to treat it as an actual number. If you type an apostrophe before the number, 1-2-3 will treat it as text. The number will be aligned on the left in the cell like any other text.

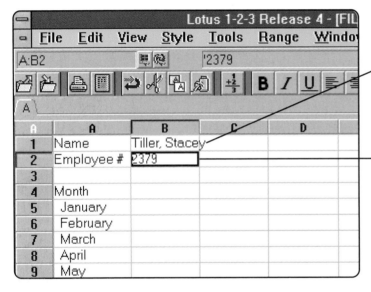

1. **Type Tiller, Stacey** in **B1** and **press** ↓ on your keyboard to enter the name in the cell and move to B2.

2. **Type '2379**. Don't forget to type the apostrophe. **Press Enter** to insert the number into B2. Notice the apostrophe doesn't show in the cell but does show in the contents box above.

Formatting the Worksheet

In this section, you will format the worksheet to have commas and two decimal places.

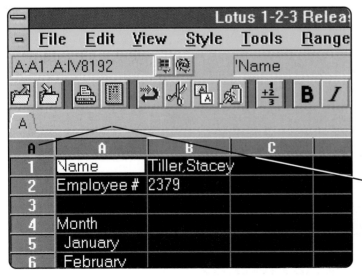

1. **Click** on the **worksheet selection button** in the left corner of the worksheet. The entire worksheet will be highlighted.

2. Click on **Automatic** in the status bar in the lower left corner of your screen. A pop-up list of number formats will appear.

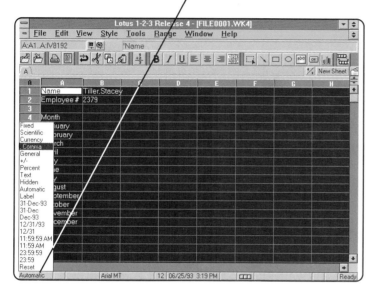

3. Click on **,Comma**. The list will disappear. The entire worksheet is now formatted to show numbers with commas.

Notice that 2 automatically appears in the status bar when you select comma as the number format. This means the numbers will appear with commas and two decimal places. You can change this, of course, by clicking on 2 and then clicking on the number of decimal places you want. However, for this example, keep it as two decimal places.

4. Click anywhere to remove the highlighting from the worksheet.

MOVING BETWEEN FILES

You cannot click on a tab to move between independent files like you did with multiple worksheets in a single file. However, moving between files is almost as easy.

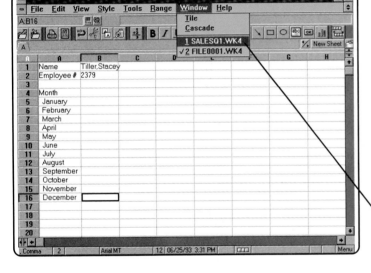

1. Click on **Window** in the menu bar. A pull-down menu will appear with the names of all open files. The files currently open are SALESQ1.WK4 and the current unnamed file, FILE0001.WK4. The number of this file depends on how many files you have opened in this work session. Your file may have a different number than shown here.

2. Click on **SALESQ1.WK4**. The SALESQ1 file will be brought to the foreground.

SHOWING TWO FILES AT THE SAME TIME

Normally only one worksheet is visible at a time. You can easily arrange the worksheets so that both can be seen. One of these arrangements is called *tiling* because the worksheets look like tiles laid side by side. You can also put files in a *cascade*, which arranges files on top of each other with only the title bars of the second and succeeding files showing.

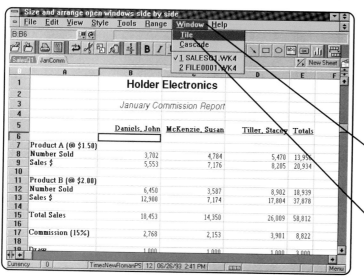

1. **Click** on **Window** in the menu bar. A pull-down menu will appear.

2. **Click** on **Tile**. The files will appear side by side on your screen.

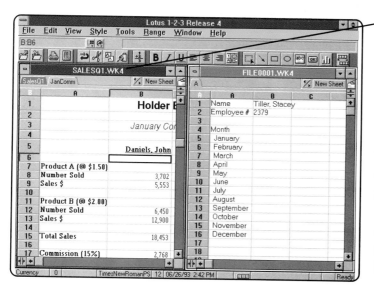

The file that was visible on your screen when you performed the tile command is the active file in the tile arrangement. The active window has the brighter-colored title bar. The colors you see on your screen depend on the colors you set in Windows. Refer to *Windows 3.1: The Visual Learning Guide* for step-by-step directions on changing the colors on your screen.

MAKING THE LINK

You do not have to have both files on your screen at the same time when you link, but it helps to see what is happening. The first step is to copy the original, or source, data.

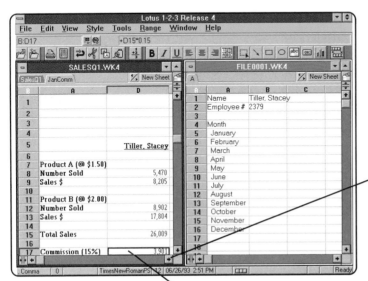

Copying the Source Data

1. **Click twice** on ➡ on the bottom scroll bar in the JanComm worksheet so you can see column D. JanComm is the *server*, which means it contains the original data.

2. **Click** on 3,901 in **D17**. (Notice that the column and row headings you froze in Chapter 15 remain in view even in a tiled worksheet.)

3. **Click** on the **Copy SmartIcon**. The data is now copied to the Clipboard.

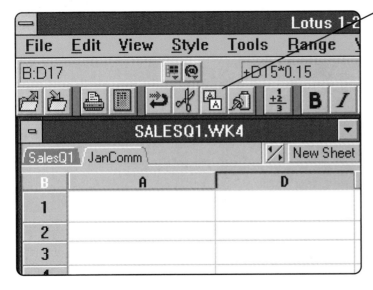

Paste-Linking the Data into the Second Worksheet

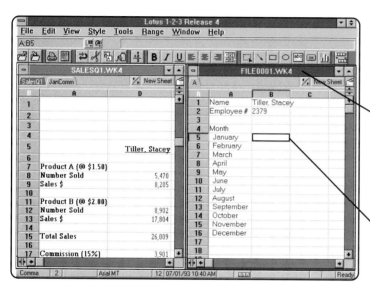

The second step in the linking process is to paste-link the data from the server file into the client file.

1. **Click** on the **title bar** of the FILE0001.WK4 file. It will change color and FILE0001 will become the active window.

2. **Click** on **B5**, the cell where you want the linked data to be.

3. **Click** on **Edit** in the menu bar. A pull-down menu will appear.

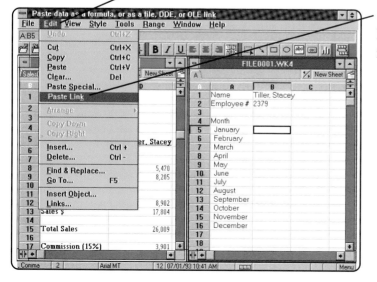

4. **Click** on **Paste Link**. The linked number will appear in B5.

Notice the number appears with two decimal places even though it had no decimal places on the server worksheet. That is because the number format you assigned to this worksheet included commas and decimal places. When the format of the server (source) and client (target) worksheets are different, the format of the client worksheet controls the appearance of the data in that worksheet.

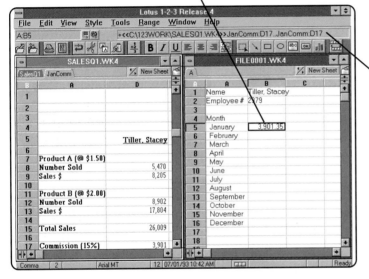

Notice the contents box. When you click on a cell, the content of the cell appears in the contents box. When the cell contains a formula, however, the formula appears in the contents box. Because this is a linked cell, the contents box reflects the link. The "+" at the beginning of the formula indicates that it is a link.

<<C:\123WORK\SALESQ1.WK4>> tells you the drive (C:), the directory (123WORK), and the name (SALESQ1.WK4) of the server worksheet. Then JanComm:D17..JanComm:D17 tells you the cell address of the original data. Since you can link ranges, the cell address shows in the range format of JanComm:D17..JanComm:D17.

TESTING THE LINK

In this section, you will have a little fun and test the link. You can do this by changing Stacey Tiller's Commission amount on the JanComm worksheet and then watching the change reflected in the linked data on FILE0001.WK4. However, you cannot simply change the Commission amount because it is the result of a formula. You must change the numbers that are part of the formula.

The formula for the Commission amount is Total Sales x 15%. Because Total Sales itself is the result of a formula, you must change one of the numbers in the Total Sales formula to change the Total Sales amount and ultimately the Commission amount. It gets complicated, doesn't it?

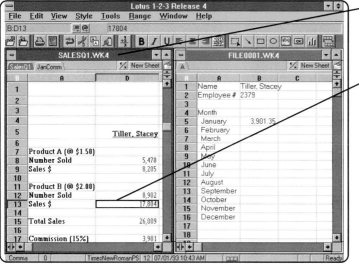

1. **Click** on the **SALESQ1 title bar** to make it the active worksheet.

2. **Click** on 17,804 in **D13**.

3. **Type 30,000.** (You don't have to type the comma. Lotus will insert it automatically.) **Press Enter** to insert the new number into D13.

Watch the Commission amount change on SALESQ1 and FILE0001!

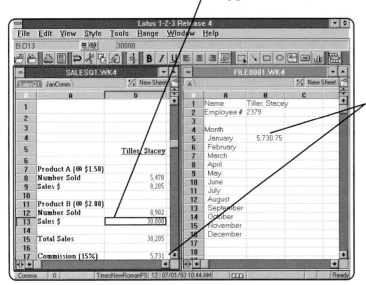

Undoing the Change

1. **Click** on the **Undo SmartIcon** to undo the change. The original numbers will appear.

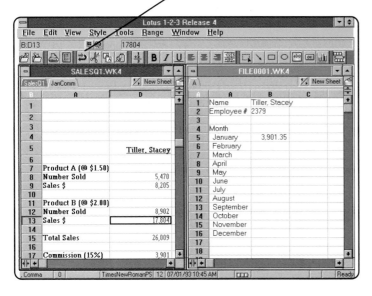

CLOSING WITHOUT SAVING

Because the unnamed FILE0001.WK4 was created only to demonstrate the linking process, you will close it without saving it.

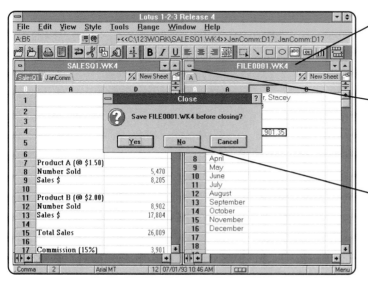

1. Click on the **FILE0001 title bar** to make it the active worksheet.

2. Click twice on the **Control menu box** (⊟) in the FILE0001 title bar. The Close dialog box will appear.

3. Click on **No**. The file will close. Because you never saved this file, the work you did in this file is gone.

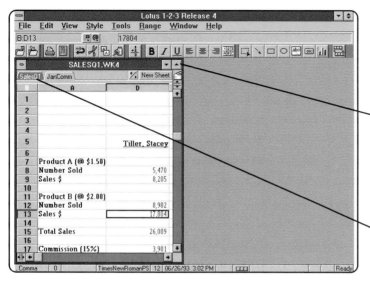

Maximizing the Remaining File

1. Click on the **Maximize button** (▲) on the SALESQ1 title bar. The worksheet will be maximized to fill the screen.

2. Click on the **SalesQ1 Tab** in preparation for Chapter 17.

Program Manager

Part IV: Charts

Creating a Bar Chart

With 1-2-3's Chart SmartIcon, you can create a chart (a graphic representation of your worksheet) automatically. You can select from a number of pre-designed formats, including 3D bar, line, pie, or area charts. Once the chart is created, you can easily change it to another type. In this chapter, you will do the following:

❖ Create a simple bar chart using the Chart SmartIcon

❖ Change the bar chart to a 3D bar chart

❖ Save the bar chart

CREATING A BAR CHART WITH THE SMARTICON

1. Open the **SALESQ1 worksheet** you created in Parts I and II. Refer to Chapter 7, "Opening a Saved File," if you need help.

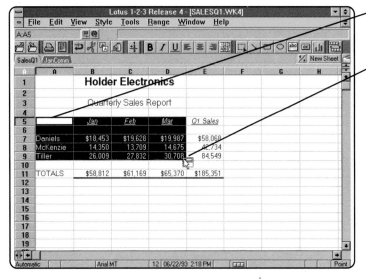

2. Move the mouse pointer to **A5**.

3. Press and hold the mouse button as you **drag** the pointer diagonally down to **D9**. **Release** the mouse button when you have highlighted the salespeoples' names and the sales data for Jan, Feb, and Mar (cells **A5 to D9**). Do not highlight the totals in column E and row 11.

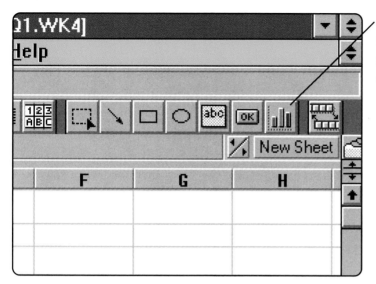

4. Click on the **Chart SmartIcon**. It should be the second tool from the right on your toolbar.

5. Place the pointer in cell A13. (*Don't click yet*). The pointer will be a crosshair and tiny bar chart. Line up the crosshair with the top left border of the cell.

6. Press and hold the mouse button as you **drag** the pointer diagonally down to **E25**. (This process tells 1-2-3 where to place your chart.) Don't be concerned that you cannot see row 25 at first. As you drag the cursor down, the screen will automatically show more rows.

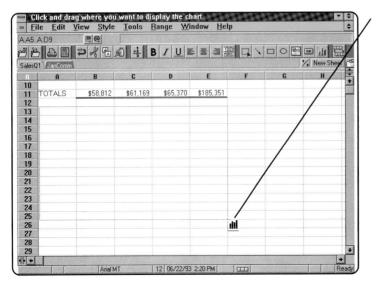

7. When cells A13 to E25 have been enclosed in the border, **release** the mouse button. A bar chart of your data will appear.

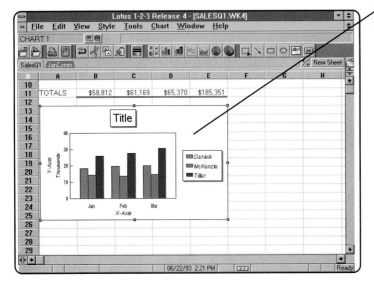

Your screen should look like the example to the left. If you cannot see the entire chart, **click** on ⬆ on the scroll bar to bring it into view.

MAKING A 3D BAR CHART

Notice that the SmartIcon tool bar has changed.

1. Click anywhere on the **chart border** to select the chart. It may already be selected from the previous exercise. Notice the black squares (or handles) around the chart perimeter. These indicate that the chart is selected.

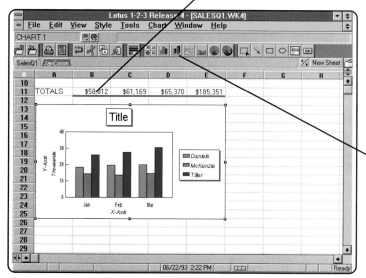

2. Click on the **3D SmartIcon** in the tool bar. The bar chart will change to a 3D look.

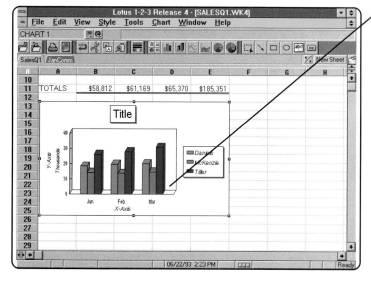

Notice that the bar chart now has a three-dimensional look.

Try clicking on the other chart SmartIcons to change the way the data is presented. Remember to click on the 3D Bar Chart SmartIcon when you're through.

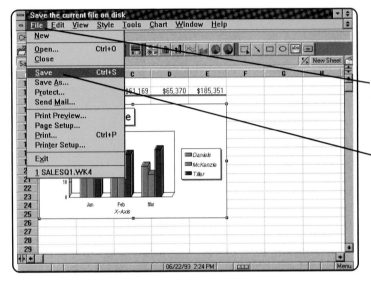

SAVING YOUR 3D BAR CHART

1. **Click** on **File** in the menu bar. A pull-down menu will appear.

2. **Click** on **Save**. The pull-down menu will disappear. Your chart is now saved as part of the SALESQ1 worksheet. If you plan to follow along with the next chapter, do not exit 1-2-3.

Working with Legends and Axis Text

A legend on a map tells you what the symbols on a map mean. Similarly, a chart legend tells you the meaning of the various colors (or shades of gray) of the chart columns. Axis text is composed of the labels on either the X or Y axis. The horizontal axis (X axis) text in the example in this chapter lists the salespeople's names. The vertical axis (Y axis) shows the amount of sales in dollars. In this chapter, you will do the following:

❖ Make a chart larger
❖ Label axes
❖ Change the orientation of text on the X axis
❖ Change the data selected for the X axis and Y axis
❖ Change the legend text
❖ Make a chart larger
❖ Move a legend to a new location
❖ Delete and restore a legend

ADDING A CHART TITLE

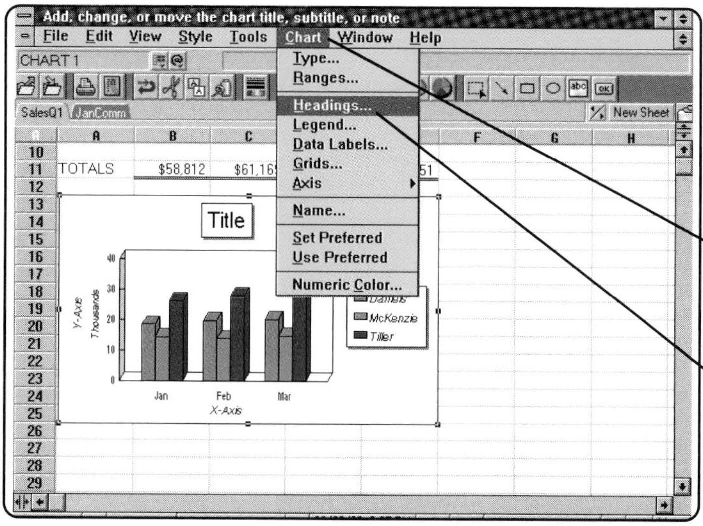

1. **Click anywhere** on the **chart border** to select the chart. The chart will be surrounded by small black handles to indicate that it has been selected. The item "Range" on the menu bar will change to "Chart."

2. **Click** on **Chart** in the menu bar. A pull-down menu will appear.

3. **Click** on **Headings**. The Headings dialog box will appear.

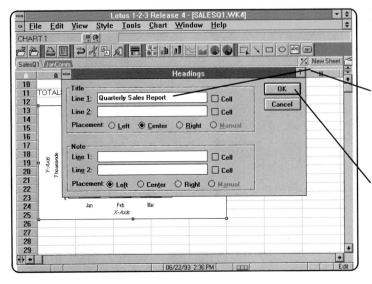

Notice that the word "title" is highlighted in Line 1 of the Title text box.

4. Type Quarterly Sales Report in the Line 1 text box. It will replace the highlighted text.

5. **Click** on **OK**.

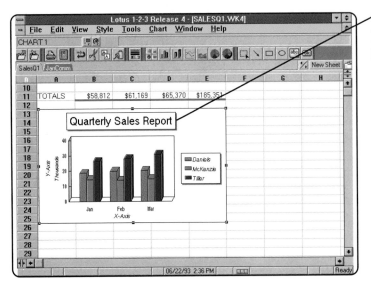

The title "Quarterly Sales Report" will appear on your bar chart.

CHANGING DATA FORMAT

Notice that the data is arranged by month (or rows) when 1-2-3 automatically created the chart. It's easy to rearrange the data. In this example, you will change the data on the X axis from months to salespeople.

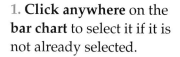

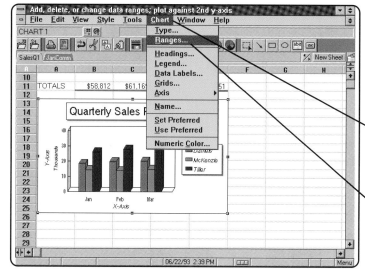

1. **Click anywhere** on the **bar chart** to select it if it is not already selected.

2. **Click** on **Chart** in the menu bar. A pull-down menu will appear.

3. **Click** on **Ranges**. The Ranges dialog box will appear.

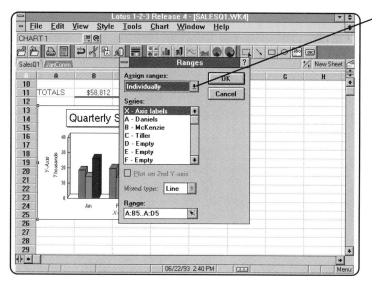

4. **Click** on the ⬇ to the right of Individually in the Assign ranges box. A drop-down list will appear.

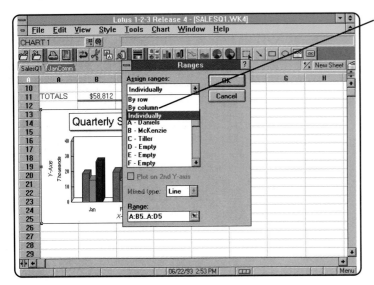

5. Click on **By column**. The drop-down list will disappear. By column will appear in the Assign ranges text box.

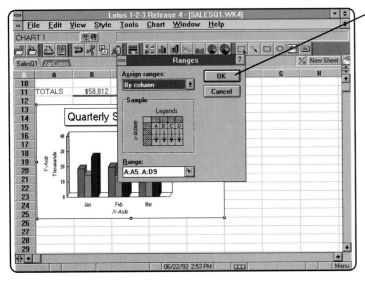

6. Click on **OK**. The Ranges dialog box will disappear. The Quarterly Sales Report chart will appear.

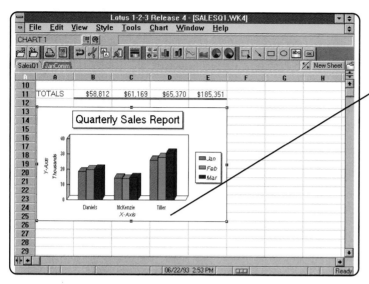

The Quarterly Sales Report chart now shows the names of the salespeople on the X Axis. The bar chart columns now represent sales by individuals.

CHANGING THE X-AXIS TITLE

In this section, you will change "X-Axis" to a more descriptive phrase.

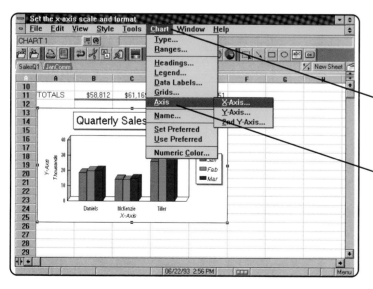

1. **Click anywhere** on the border of the **bar chart** if it is not already selected.

2. **Click** on **Chart** in the menu bar. A pull-down menu will appear.

3. **Click** on **Axis**. A second menu will appear.

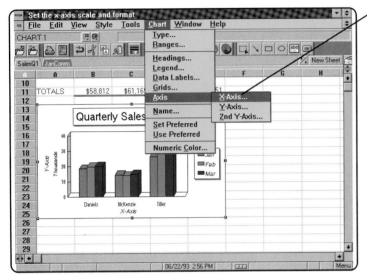

4. Click on **X-Axis**. The X-Axis text box will appear.

X-Axis will be highlighted in the Axis title text box.

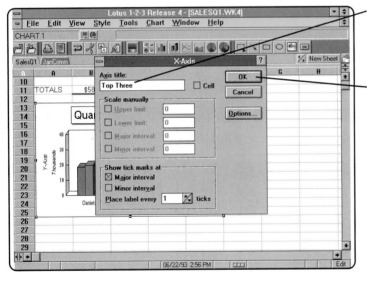

5. Type Top Three in the Axis title text box. It will replace the highlighted text.

6. Click on **OK**. The bar chart will appear.

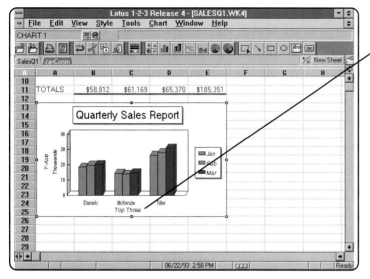

Notice that the label "Top Three" has replaced "X-Axis" in the SalesQ1 "Quarterly Sales Report."

CHANGING THE Y-AXIS TITLE

In this section, you will add the label "Dollars" to explain that the numbers on the Y-axis scale represent money.

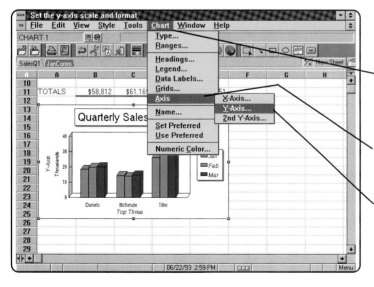

1. **Click anywhere** on the **chart border** to select it.

2. **Click** on **Chart** in the menu bar. A pull-down menu will appear.

3. **Click** on **Axis**. A second menu will appear.

4. **Click** on **Y-Axis**. The Y-Axis menu will appear.

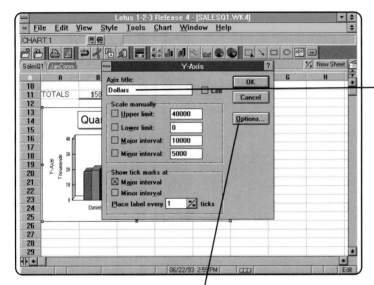

The Y-Axis range will be highlighted in the Axis title text box.

5. **Type Dollars** in the Axis title box. It will replace the highlighted text.

CHANGING GRAPH UNITS AND INTERVALS

In this section, you will change the dollar interval from 10,000 to 5,000.

1. **Click** on **Options** in the Axes dialog box. The Options dialog box will appear.

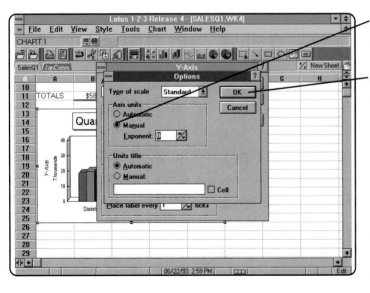

2. **Click** on **Manual** to insert a dot in the circle.

3. **Click** on **OK**. The Y-Axis dialog box will reappear.

4. Click on **Major interval** to place an × in the box. The 10000 figure will become highlighted and the cursor will flash in the Major interval text box.

5. **Type** 5000.

6. **Click** on **OK**. The Quarterly Sales Report will appear.

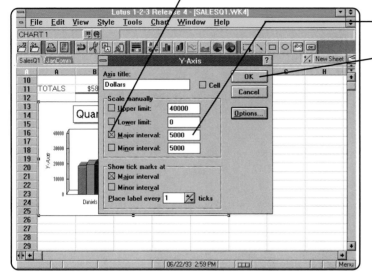

Notice that the dollar amounts are now shown in intervals of 5000.

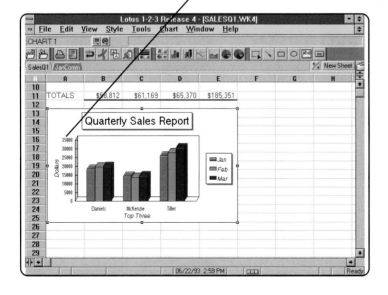

CHANGING LEGEND TEXT

The legend text is taken from the worksheet. To change the legend text, change the worksheet text.

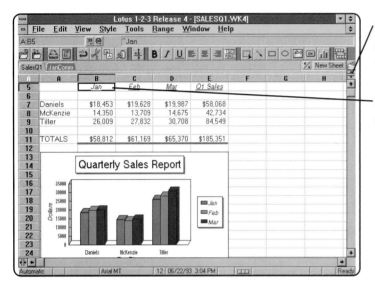

1. **Click** on the ⬆ on the scroll bar to bring the worksheet into view.

2. **Click twice** on **Jan** to select cell B5 for editing.

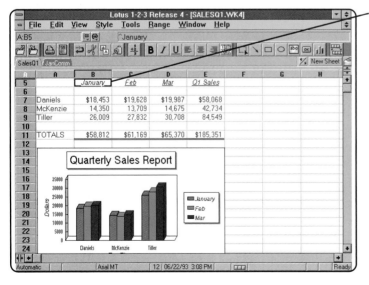

3. **Click twice** to highlight the contents of the cell. **Type January**. It will replace "Jan."

4. **Press** the **Enter** key to enter the text and to highlight the cell. Leave the mouse pointer in the cell.

5. Press and hold the mouse button and drag it over to cell **D5** to highlight Feb and Mar.

6. Release the mouse button when you have highlighted C5 through D5.

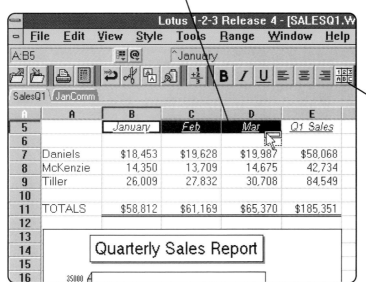

7. Click on the **Fill by Example SmartIcon**. The headings "Feb" and "Mar" will automatically change to "February" and "March." The change will appear in the legend on the chart at the same time.

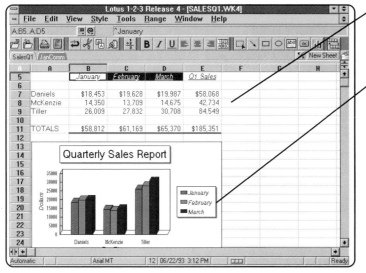

8. Click anywhere on the **worksheet** to remove the highlighting.

Notice the legend with the new changes.

ENLARGING A GRAPH

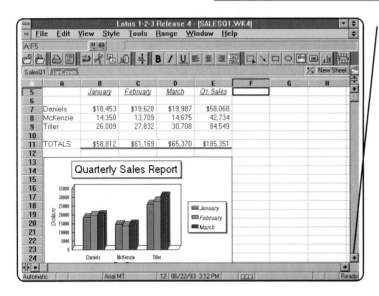

1. Click repeatedly on the ⬇ on the scroll bar to bring the chart into full view.

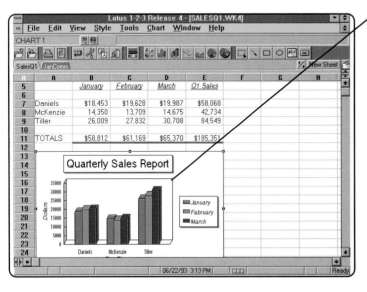

2. Click anywhere on the **chart border** to select it. Selection handles will appear on the border.

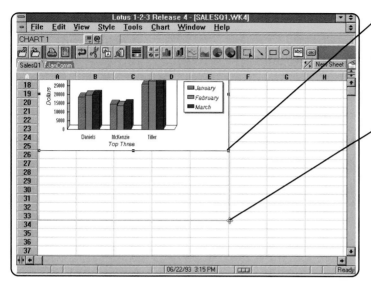

3. Place the **mouse arrow** on the **selection box** at the bottom right corner of the chart. The mouse arrow will turn into a double arrow.

4. Press and hold the mouse button and drag the border down to **row 33**. You may have to fiddle with this to get it to line up.

5. Release the mouse button. The chart will expand to fill the space.

MOVING A LEGEND

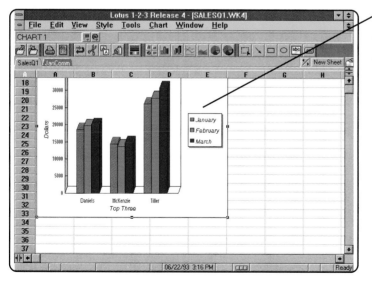

1. Click on the **chart** to select it if it is not already highlighted.

2. Click on **Chart** in the menu bar. A pull-down menu will appear.

3. Click on **Legend**. A Legend text box will appear.

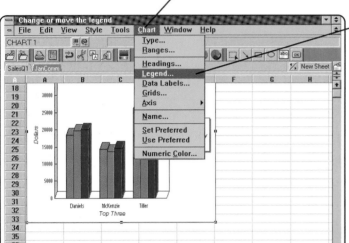

4. Click on **Below plot** to insert a dot in the circle.

5. Click on **OK**. The legend will now appear at the bottom of the Quarterly Sales Report Chart.

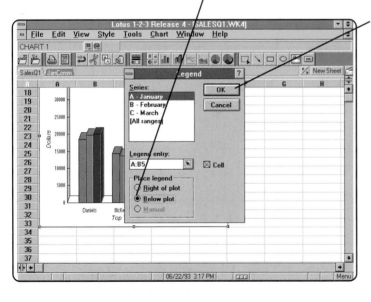

DELETING A LEGEND

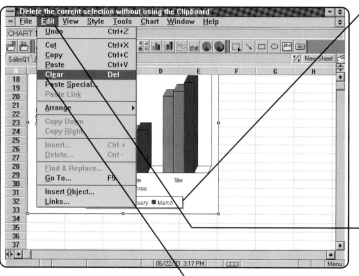

1. Click on the **border** of the **legend box**. Small, black boxes will appear in the corners of the border to indicate that the legend has been selected. If you get boxes around the text, click the mouse arrow on the border of the legend box until you get the correct boxes.

2. Click on **Edit** in the graph menu bar. A pull-down menu will appear.

3. Click on **Clear**. The legend will disappear.

You will restore the legend in the next section.

RESTORING A LEGEND

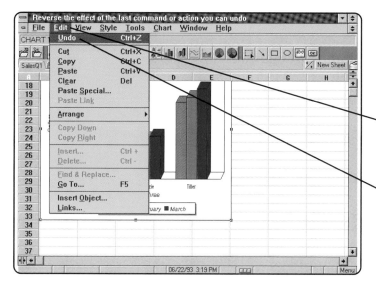

This procedure works only if deleting the legend was the last thing you did.

1. Click on **Edit** in the menu bar. A pull-down menu will appear.

2. Click on **Undo**. The pull-down menu will disappear and the legend box will reappear at the bottom of the chart.

SAVING CHANGES IN A CHART

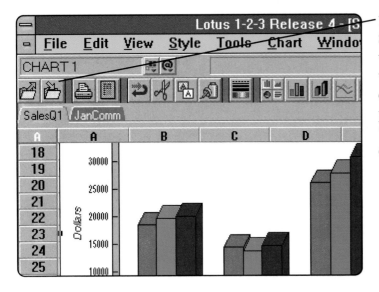

1. **Click** on the **Save SmartIcon**. An hourglass will appear briefly and the worksheet with the edited chart is now saved. If you plan to go on to Chapter 19, "Printing Charts," do not exit 1-2-3.

Printing Charts

You can print a chart by itself or on the same page with a worksheet. You can also print a chart and a worksheet sideways. Printing sideways is called printing in landscape orientation. In this chapter, you will do the following:

❖ Print a chart

❖ Print a chart and a worksheet on the same page

❖ Preview and print a chart and a worksheet sideways (in landscape orientation)

PRINTING A CHART

In this section, you will print only a chart.

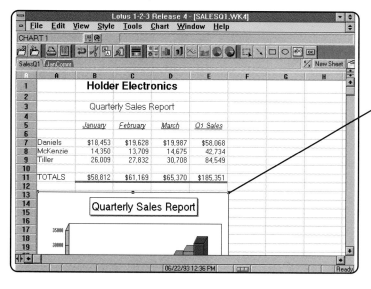

1. **Open** the **SALESQ1 worksheet** with Chart 1 if it is not already on your screen.

2. **Click** on the **border** of the **chart** to select it.

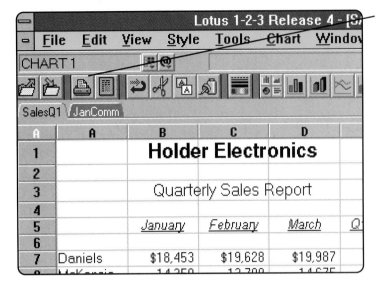

3. Click on the **Print SmartIcon**. The Print dialog box will appear.

Notice that Chart 1 shows in the Selected chart box.

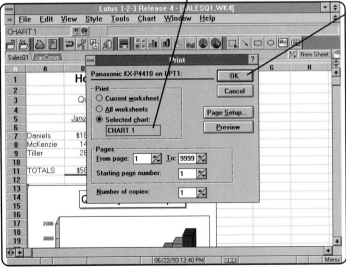

4. Click on **OK**. The Printing message box will appear. The SALESQ1 CHART 1 will be printed.

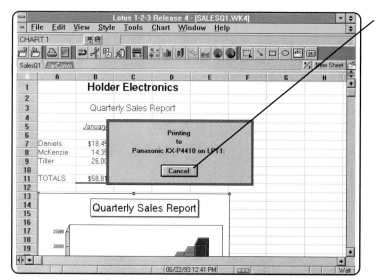

5. If you change your mind, **click** on **Cancel**.

PRINTING A WORKSHEET AND A CHART AT THE SAME TIME

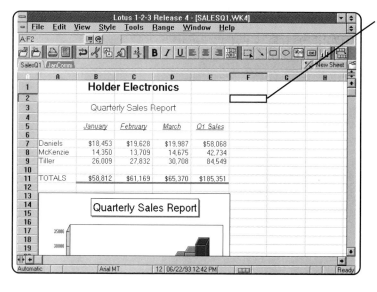

1. Click anywhere on the **worksheet**. The chart will no longer be selected.

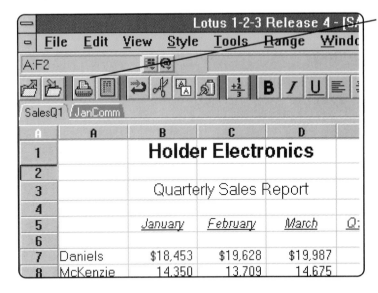

2. Click on the **Print SmartIcon**. The Print dialog box will appear.

3. Click on **Current worksheet** if it is not already selected.

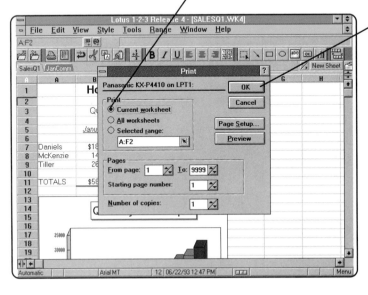

4. Click on **OK**. The Printing message box will appear. The SALESQ1 worksheet and the chart will be printed together on the same page.

5. If you change your mind, **click** on **Cancel** in the Printing message box.

PRINTING A WORKSHEET AND A CHART SIDEWAYS

There may be a time when you will want to print both a worksheet and a chart sideways (in *landscape* orientation) on your paper, especially if your worksheet is quite wide.

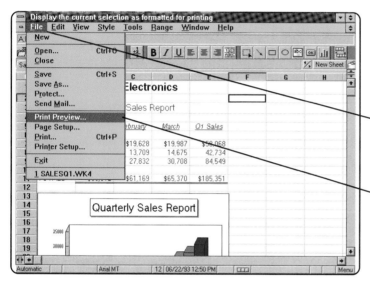

1. Click on **File** in the menu bar. A pull-down menu will appear.

2. Click on **Print Preview**. The Print Preview screen will appear.

Notice that Current worksheet is automatically selected.

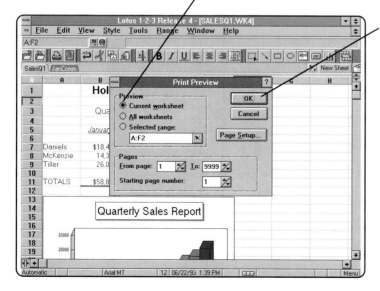

3. Click on **OK**. The preview screen will appear.

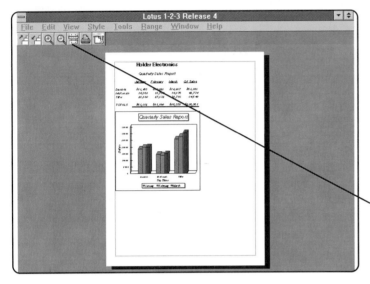

Most documents are normally printed in *portrait* orientation, with the short side of the paper at the top. This is what you will see the first time you select the Print Preview option. This preview is an example of a portrait orientation.

4. Click on the **Page setup SmartIcon**. The Page Setup dialog box will appear.

5. Click on **Landscape** in the Orientation box to place a dot in the circle.

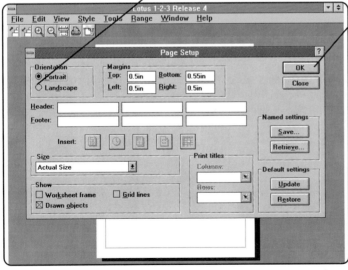

6. Click on **OK**. The preview screen will reappear. This time the page view will appear in landscape orientation.

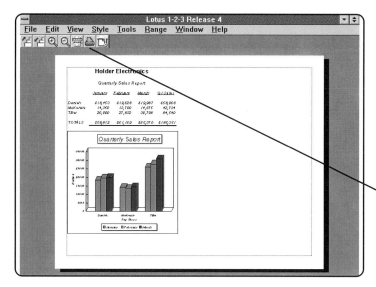

Landscape printing means printing with the long side of the paper on top. Landscape printing is often used to print financial worksheets and charts that are too wide to be printed in portrait.

7. Click on the **Print SmartIcon**. The Print dialog box will appear.

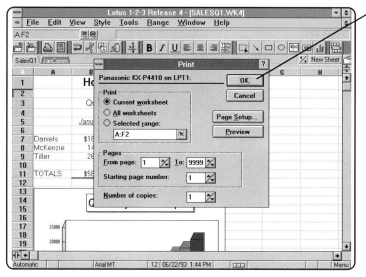

8. Click on **OK**. The worksheet and chart will be printed sideways.

Switching Back to Portrait Printing

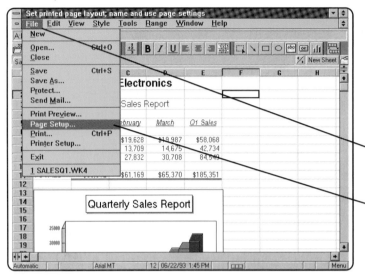

It is a good idea to switch back to portrait printing at this time. Otherwise, the next time you print the worksheet, it will be printed sideways.

1. Click on **File**. A pull-down menu will appear.

2. Click on **Page Setup**. The Page Setup dialog box will appear.

3. Click on **Portrait** in the Orientation box to place a dot in the circle.

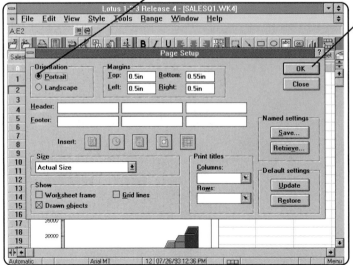

4. Click on **OK**. The SALESQ1 screen will appear.

If you are going to Chapter 20, you need not exit or save at this time.

Naming, Copying, and Deleting a Chart

As you will see, naming a chart in Lotus 1-2-3 is as easy as 1-2-3 clicks of the mouse. Not only that, you can give the chart a name that has more than one word. If you have a large worksheet, you may want to remove the chart from the worksheet and store it in its own file. A chart saved to its own separate file continues to be linked to the worksheet. Any changes made in the worksheet will be automatically reflected in this chart. You can also restore a deleted chart to your worksheet at any time. In this chapter, you will do the following:

❖ Save a chart to a separate file

❖ Delete the chart from the worksheet

❖ Restore the chart to the worksheet

NAMING A CHART

1. **Click** on the **outside border** of the **chart** to select it. The chart will become surrounded by black handles.

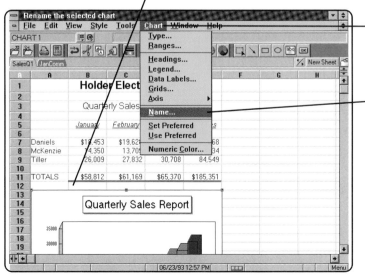

2. **Click** on **Chart** in the main menu. A pull-down menu will appear.

3. **Click** on **Name**. The Name dialog box will appear. Chart 1 will be highlighted in the Chart name text box.

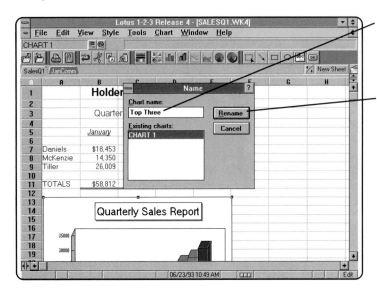

4. Type Top Three in the Chart name text box. It will replace the highlighted text.

5. Click on **Rename**. The Top Three worksheet chart window will appear.

Notice that the selected chart is now labeled TOP THREE in the Selection Indicator box.

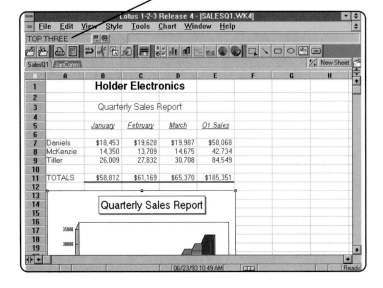

COPYING A CHART TO ANOTHER WORKSHEET

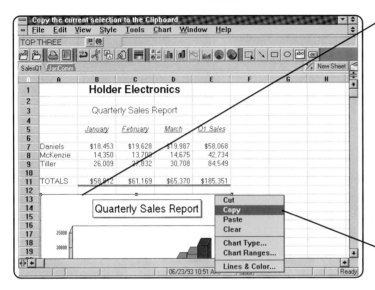

1. **Click** on the **border** of the chart if it does not already have selection boxes around the border. Keep the mouse pointer in the chart.

2. **Click** on the **right** mouse button. A quick menu will appear. (If it doesn't, make sure the chart is highlighted).

3. **Click** on **Copy**. The quick menu will disappear.

4. **Click** on **File** in the menu bar. A pull-down menu will appear.

5. **Click** on **New**. A new worksheet will appear.

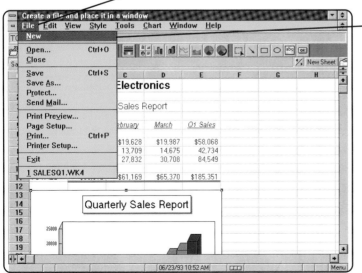

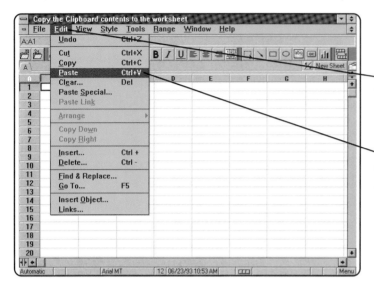

6. Click on **A1** if it is not already selected.

7. Click on **Edit** in the menu bar. A pull-down menu will appear.

8. Click on **Paste**. The chart will appear on the new worksheet beginning in A1.

CLOSING WITHOUT SAVING

In this example, you will close this new file without saving.

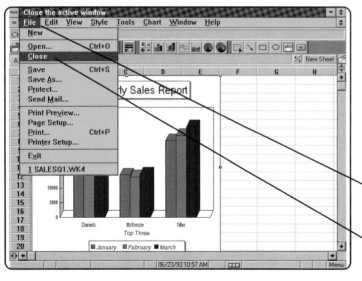

However, you can save this chart if you want to by clicking on Save and then giving the file a name. It will be linked to the SalesQ1 worksheet. Any changes made to SalesQ1 will also be made in this new chart.

1. Click on **File**. A pull-down menu will appear.

2. Click on **Close**. The Close dialog box will appear.

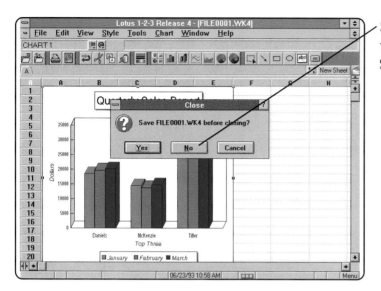

3. **Click** on **No**. The worksheet will close and the SalesQ1 window will appear.

DELETING AND RESTORING A CHART

In this example, you will delete the chart, Top Three, and then restore it.

Deleting the Chart

Because you want to restore the chart after deleting it, make certain that you follow these instructions step by step.

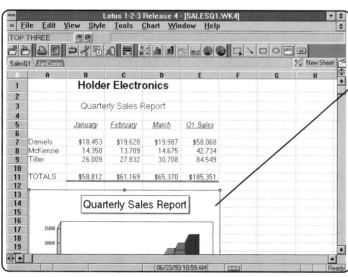

1. **Click** on the **outside border** of the **chart** to select it. It will be surrounded by black handles.

2. **Press** the **Delete** key on your keyboard. The chart will disappear. If you get a message that says you cannot delete, you have not selected the outside border. Try again.

RESTORING THE CHART WITH THE UNDO COMMAND

1. Click on **Edit** in the menu bar. A pull-down menu will appear.

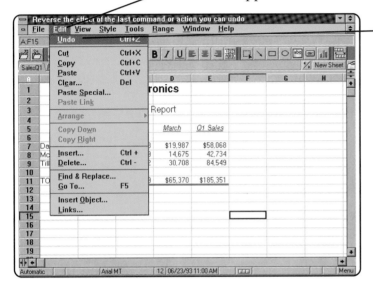

2. Click on **Undo**. The chart will be restored.

Note: If you make a change after pressing the Delete key and before clicking on Edit-Undo, your chart will not be restored.

Notice that TOP THREE has been restored.

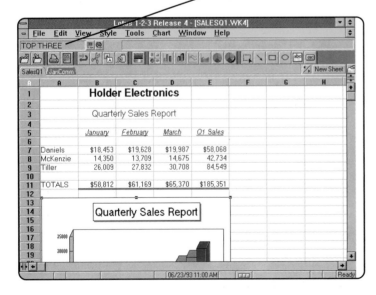

Do not exit or close if you plan to follow along with the next chapter.

Adding and Editing Chart Text and Arrows

In Lotus 1-2-3, the chart headings text comes with the territory. You can change and move it only where it will let you. However, you can add additional text and place it anywhere on the chart by using the text block drawing tool. Similarly, arrows and other shapes can be added and placed anywhere on the chart. In this chapter, you will do the following:

❖ Edit the headings text

❖ Add a footnote

❖ Add new text with the text block tool

❖ Draw an arrow to point to the highest column on the chart

EDITING HEADING TEXT

1. Click on the **outside border** of the **chart** to select it. It will be surrounded with black handles. The Chart tool bar will appear.

2. Click on **Chart** in the menu bar. A pull-down menu will appear.

3. Click on **Headings**. The Headings dialog box will appear. The chart title will be highlighted in Line 1 of the Title text box.

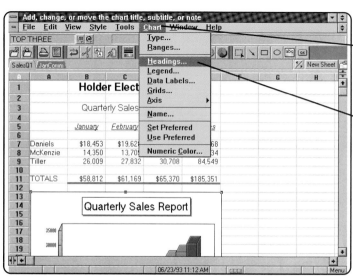

4. Click on **Line 2** of the Title text box to set the cursor.

5. Type Top Three Producers in the text box.

6. Click on **OK**.

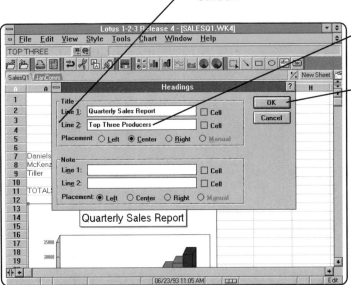

Notice that Top Three Producers has been added to the Quarterly Sales Report heading.

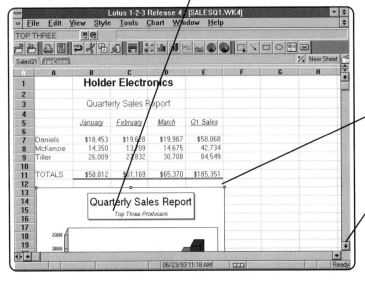

ADDING A FOOTNOTE

1. Click on the chart **border** if it does not already have black selection handles around it.

2. Click on the ⬇ repeatedly to scroll the entire chart into view.

3. Click on **Chart** in the menu bar. A pull-down menu will appear.

4. Click on **Headings**. The Headings dialog box will appear. The chart title will be highlighted in Line 1 of the Title text box.

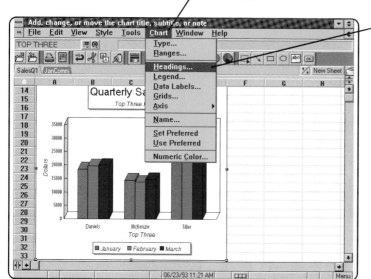

5. Click on **Line 1** of the **Note** text box to set the cursor.

6. Type San Diego Area in the text box.

7. Click on **Line 2** of the **Note** text box to set the cursor.

8. Type 1993 in the text box.

9. Click on **Center** in the Placement line to put a dot in the circle.

10. Click on **OK**. The Top Three chart will reappear. The footnotes you just typed will appear in the center of the chart in a box.

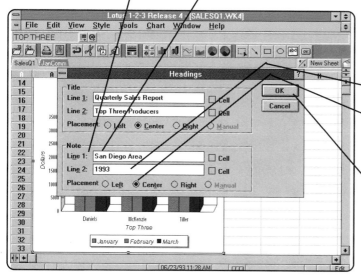

ADDING TEXT WITH THE TEXT BLOCK SMARTICON

1. Click on the chart **border** if it does not already have black selection handles around it.

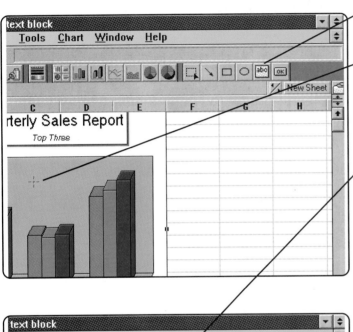

2. Click on the **Text Block SmartIcon**.

3. Place the **mouse pointer** at the spot where you want the text block to begin. Notice that the cursor changes to a crosshair.

4. Press and hold the mouse button and **drag** the cursor down and over to **form a rectangle**. **Warning:** Do not release the mouse button until you have finished. Otherwise, you will have a mess on your hands. (If you make a mistake, release the mouse button. Click on the new text block until you see black handles, press the Delete key on your keyboard, and start over with step 2).

5. Release the mouse button when you have drawn a text block approximately like this one. As long as you hold the mouse button down, you can work with the shape until it looks right to you.

Notice that the cursor is flashing in the newly created text block.

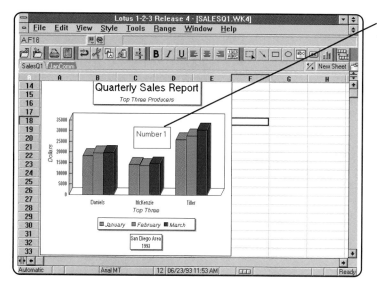

6. **Type Number 1** in the text block.

RESIZING THE TEXT BLOCK

1. **Click anywhere outside** the **text block**.

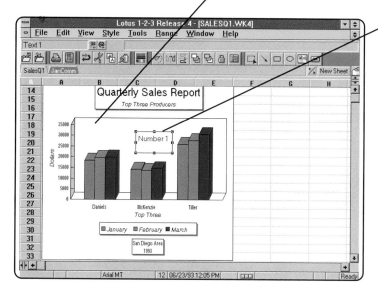

2. **Click** on **Number 1**. The text block will be surrounded with black handles.

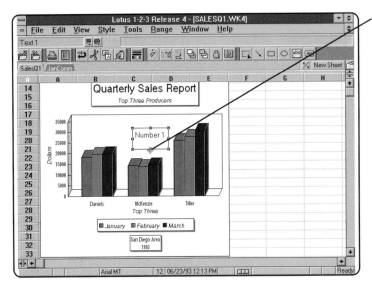

3. **Place** the **mouse pointer** on the **center bottom handle**. The pointer will change to a white cross.

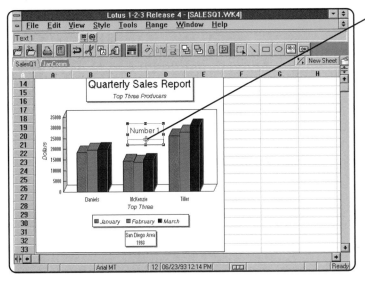

4. **Press and hold** the **mouse button** and **drag** the handle up to shrink the text block. When the block looks about right, **release** the mouse button. This is an "eyeball" affair, so don't worry if yours doesn't look like this one.

MOVING THE TEXT BLOCK

1. **Click** on the **text block** to select it if it is not already selected. It will be surrounded with black handles. Click until you can see black squares on the text block border.

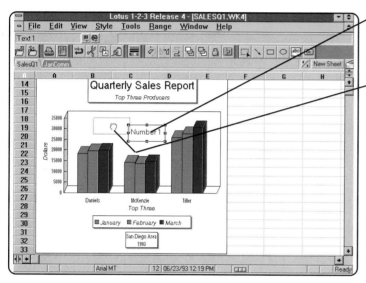

2. **Place** the **mouse pointer** in the **middle** of the text block.

3. **Press and hold** the mouse button as you **drag** the **block** to the left. An outline of the block will form and move as you move the mouse. The pointer will turn into a little hand. When the text block is about where you want it, release the mouse button. The text block will move to the new position. Neat, huh?

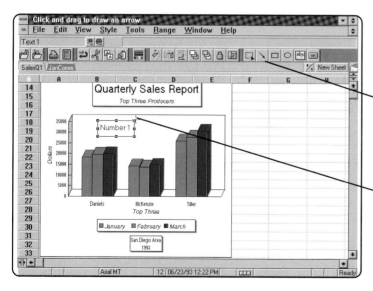

DRAWING AN ARROW

1. **Click** on the **Arrow SmartIcon** on the tool bar. The cursor will become a crosshair.

2. **Place** the **crosshair** in the upper right corner of the new text block.

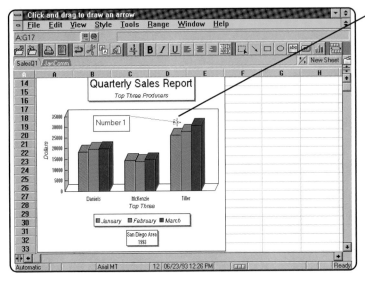

3. Press and hold the mouse button as you **drag** the **crosshair** to a spot where it is pointing to the tallest column representing Tiller's March sales figures. (**Note:** The arrow line may look jagged on your screen. It will print correctly).

Do not release the mouse button until you have completed the line or you will end up with a very short, weird-looking arrow! If you make a mistake, press the Delete key on your keyboard and repeat step 1.

4. Release the **mouse button**. The arrow will appear, arrowhead and all. Arrow-drawing can be tricky at first. You may have to make several attempts to get an arrow drawn the way you want it.

If you plan to go on to Chapter 22, do not close the file.

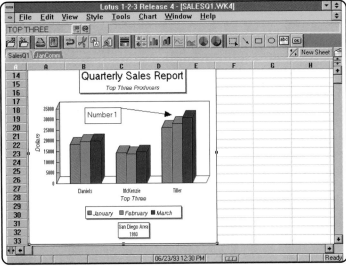

Styling a Chart

In Lotus 1-2-3, there are many ways you can make your chart more attractive. You can change the text fonts, background color, and patterns, and even add designer frames around text blocks. You are limited only by your own imagination. In this chapter, you will do the following:

❖ Change the font in a text block

❖ Add a designer frame to the title text block

❖ Change the background pattern in the title text block

CHANGING A FONT IN A TEXT BLOCK

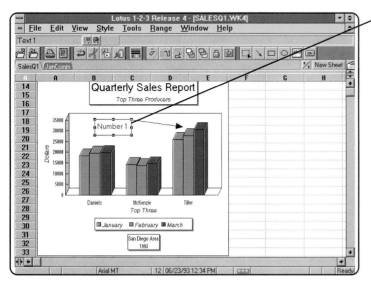

1. **Place** the **mouse pointer** in the **Number 1 text block**.

2. **Click** on **Number 1**. The text block will be surrounded with black handles.

3. Click on **Style** in the menu bar. A pull-down menu will appear.

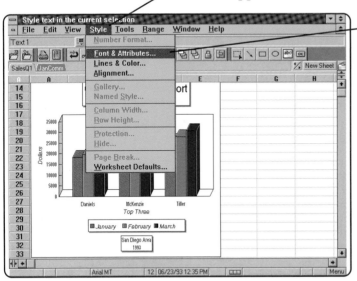

4. Click on **Font & Attributes**. The Font & Attributes dialog box will appear.

Note: You can repeat the steps in this section to change the fonts on any text in the chart.

5. Click repeatedly on the ⬇ to the right of the list of fonts to scroll down the list until the font you want to select comes into view. (In this example, we are using Times New Roman. You may have a different list of fonts than the ones shown here.)

6. Click on **Times New Roman**. Times New Roman will appear in the Font text box.

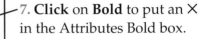

7. Click on **Bold** to put an ✕ in the Attributes Bold box.

8. Click on **OK**. The Font & Attributes dialog box will disappear. The font for Number 1 is now Times New Roman, Bold.

ADDING A DESIGNER FRAME

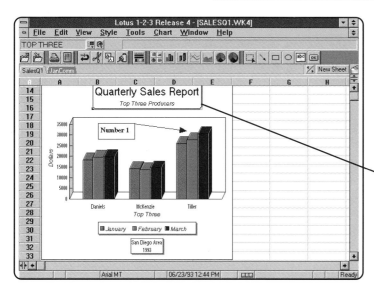

You can place a designer frame around the entire chart or around any of the text block elements on the chart. In this example, you will put a designer frame around the title text block.

1. Click on the **edge** of the **title text block** to select it. Black handles will appear on each corner of the block.

2. Click on **Style** in the menu bar. A pull-down menu will appear.

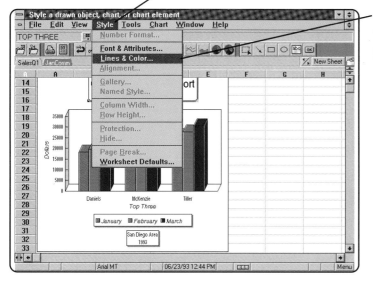

3. Click on **Lines & Color**. The Lines & Color dialog box will appear.

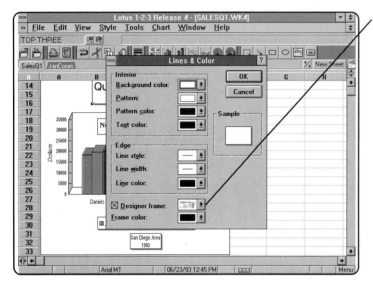

4. Click on the ⬇ to the right of the designer Frame selection box. A pop-up dialog box of frame choices will appear.

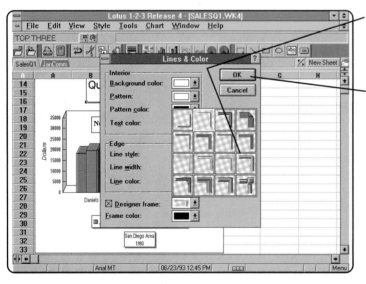

5. Click on the **designer frame** on the **far right side** of the third row of choices.

6. Click on **OK**. The pop-up menu will disappear. The text "Quarterly Sales Report" will be surrounded by a frame.

CHANGING THE BACKGROUND PATTERN ON THE CHART TITLE

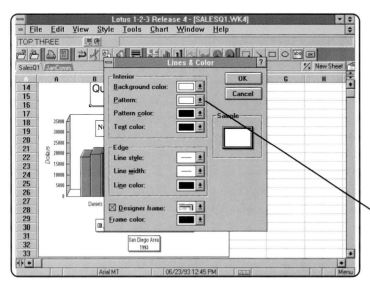

1. **Click** on the inside of the frame around **Quarterly Sales Report** until you see selection handles appear in the corners of the frame.

2. **Repeat steps 2 and 3** in the preceding section to open the Lines & Color dialog box.

3. **Click** on the ⬇ to the right of the **Patterns text box**. A drop-down box of pattern choices will appear.

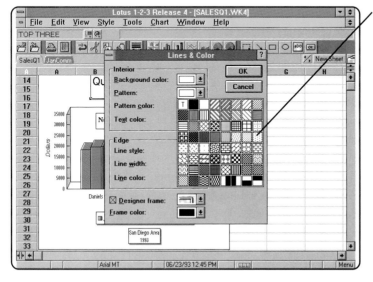

4. **Click** on the **pattern** on the **far right** of the **fourth row** of choices. The box will disappear. You will see the selected pattern in the sample box in the dialog box.

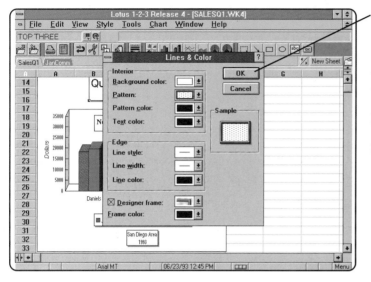

5. Click on **OK**. The Lines & Colors dialog box will disappear. You have now changed the appearance of the chart title. A new bold font, a designer frame, and a background pattern all give it a new look.

RESTORING THE ORIGINAL STYLE

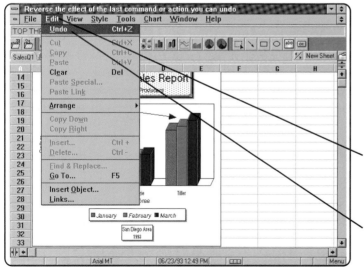

If you don't like the pattern, you can undo it. Make certain that you haven't completed another action prior to step 1 below or the Undo command won't work.

1. Click on **Edit** in the menu bar. A pull-down menu will appear.

2. Click on **Undo**. Bingo! The pattern has disappeared.

Program Manager

Part V: Special Features

Dynamic Data Exchange

Another terrific feature of Windows is that you can *link* a worksheet chart into a word-processed document. When a worksheet chart is linked to a word-processed document, *any changes made in the worksheet chart are automatically reflected* in the document. This feature is called *Dynamic Data Exchange*. In this chapter, you will do the following:

❖ Copy a chart to the Windows Clipboard

❖ Open a word-processed document file

❖ Paste-link a chart to a word-processed document

❖ Observe the link in action

THE COPY-AND-LINK PROCESS

The copy-and-link process described in this chapter consists of four stages:

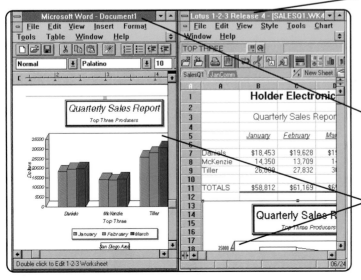

Stage 1: Copying the 1-2-3 chart to the windows Clipboard

Stage 2: Keeping 1-2-3 running in the background

Stage 3: Opening a word-processed document into which you will paste-link the chart

Stage 4: Paste-linking a copy of the 1-2-3 chart from the Clipboard into the word-processed document

Copying a Chart to the Windows Clipboard

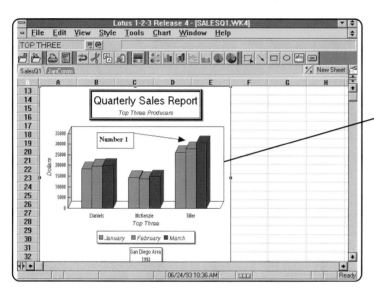

1. **Open** the **SALESQ1 worksheet** containing the Top Three chart you created in Part IV.

2 **Click anywhere** on the **border** of the **chart** to select it.

3. **Click** on **Edit** in the menu bar. A pull-down menu will appear.

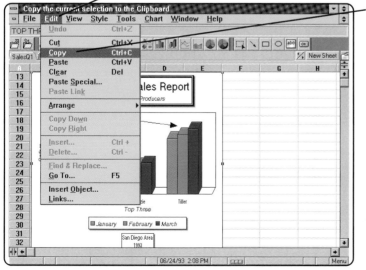

4. **Click** on **Copy**. The chart will be copied to the Clipboard. The chart is now ready to be linked to a word-processed document file.

Running 1-2-3 in the Background

To link the Top Three chart to a word-processed document, 1-2-3 must be running in the background.

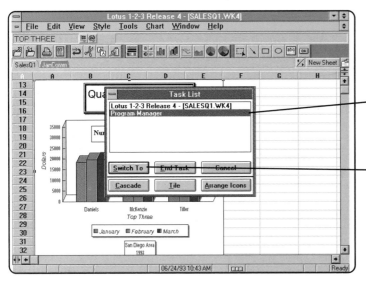

1. **Press and hold** the **Ctrl** key and **press** the **Esc** key (Ctrl + Esc.) The Task List dialog box will appear.

2. **Click** on **Program Manager**. It will become highlighted.

3. **Click** on **Switch To**. The Program Manager window will appear in the foreground. The 1-2-3 window will move to the background.

Opening a Word-Processed Document

We used Word for Windows 2 as the word processing program in this example. However, WordPerfect for Windows and Ami Pro link charts in much the same way.

1. **Click twice** on the **icon** of the word processing program you use.

Linking the Chart

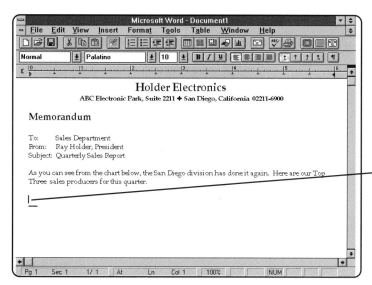

This example shows the chart being linked to a memo. However, you can link into a blank document file if you don't want to bother typing the memo text.

1. Move the cursor to the spot on the document where you want to paste-link the copy of the Top Three chart.

2. Click on **Edit** in the menu bar. A pull-down menu will appear.

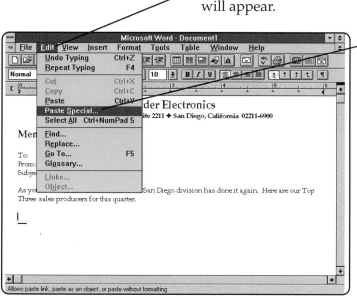

3. Click on **Paste Special**. The Paste Special dialog box will appear.

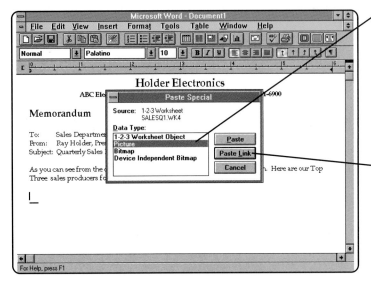

4. Click on **Picture** in the Data Type dialog box. (You are choosing Picture instead of 1-2-3 Worksheet Object because 1-2-3 Worksheet Object does not give you the Paste Link option.)

5. Click on **Paste Link**. "Top Three" will appear in the word-processed document.

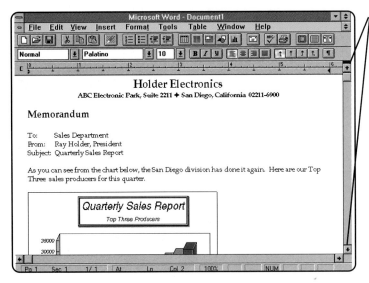

6. Click repeatedly on the ⬆ or ⬇ on the scroll bar to bring the chart into view.

CENTERING THE CHART IN THE WORD-PROCESSED DOCUMENT

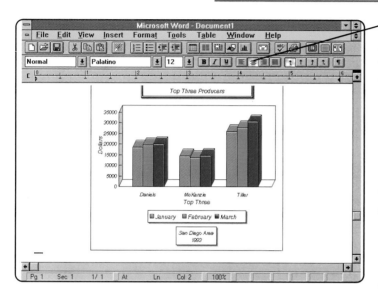

1. Click on the **Center icon** in the icon bar. The chart will move to the center of the page.

SIZING THE CHART IN THE WORD-PROCESSED DOCUMENT

1. Click repeatedly on the ⬇ on the scroll bar to bring the lower border of the chart into view if it isn't already.

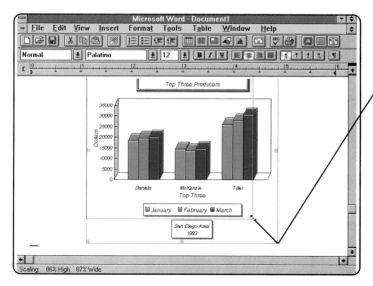

2. Click on the **chart** to select it. It will be surrounded by black handles.

3. Place the mouse arrow on the handle at the right corner of the chart. The mouse arrow will turn into a double arrow. **Press** and hold the mouse button and drag the border up to make the chart smaller.

4. Release the mouse button. The chart will shrink.

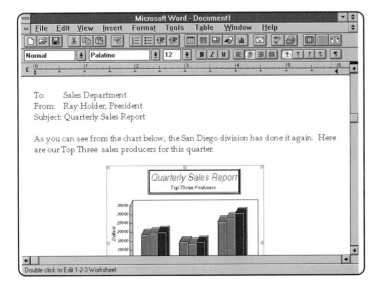

Notice that the chart is now smaller and centered in the memo.

VIEWING 1-2-3 AND WORD SIDE BY SIDE

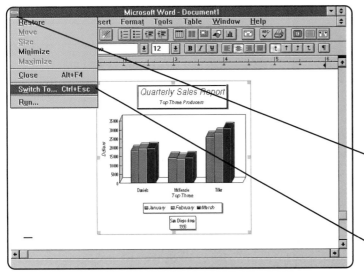

To really appreciate how a link works, you must see it in action. In this section, you will place the 1-2-3 worksheet and the word-processed memo side by side (called *tiling*).

1. **Click** on the **Control menu box** (⊟) on the left side of the title bar. A pull-down menu will appear.

2. **Click** on **Switch To**. The Task List dialog box will appear.

Caution: To place (tile) two programs side by side, no other programs can be running except Program Manager, which must be minimized. If your Task List shows programs other than the three listed in the example here, close them before proceeding.

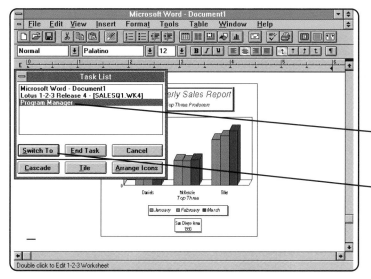

Exception: If you have ATM or Print Cache 3.1 running, they may show up on your Task List, but they do not need to be closed.

3. **Click** on **Program Manager.**

4. **Click** on **Switch To.** The Program Manager window will appear.

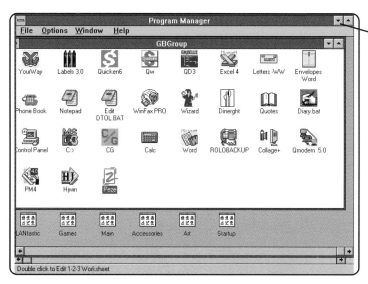

5. **Click** on the **Minimize button** (▼) to the right of the Program Manager title bar. The Program Manager screen will disappear. The Word Document window will move to the foreground.

6. Click on the **Control menu box** (⊟) to the left of the Word title bar. A pull-down menu will appear.

7. Click on **Switch To**. The Task List dialog box will appear.

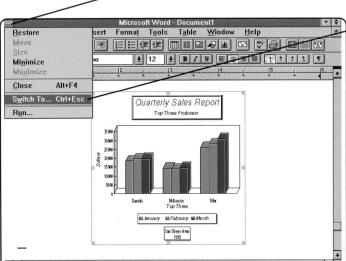

8. Click on **Lotus 1-2-3 Release 4.**

9. Click on **Tile**. The two windows, Word and 1-2-3, will appear side by side.

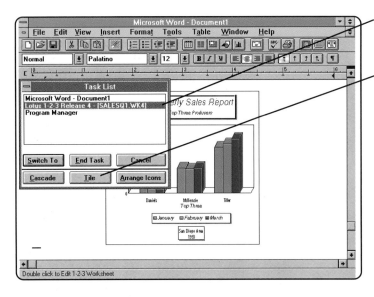

Enlarging the Two Windows

To get a better view, you must enlarge both windows.

1. **Place** the **pointer** on the **bottom edge** of the **Word window**. The pointer will turn into a two-headed arrow.

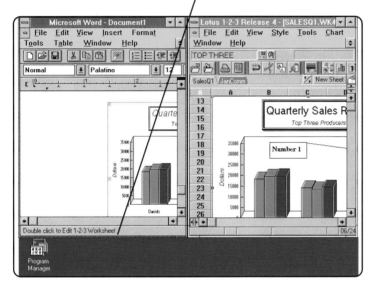

2. **Press and hold** the mouse button as you **drag** the **edge** of the window to the **bottom** of the screen. As you drag, the border of the window will expand. It's okay to cover the Program Manager icon.

3. **Release** the mouse button. The Word window will expand to the bottom of the screen.

4. **Repeat steps 1 to 3** to enlarge the 1-2-3 window.

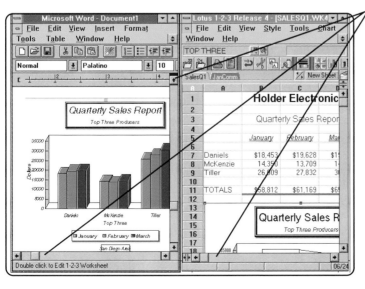

5. **Click repeatedly** on the **scroll bar arrows** on *both windows* until your view approximates the one in this example. You want to be able to see the chart columns on the word processing window and, at the same time, see the worksheet sales figures on the 1-2-3 window. You may have to fiddle with the two scroll bars in each window to get there. Tiling can be frustrating, so keep trying until you get it right.

TESTING THE LINK

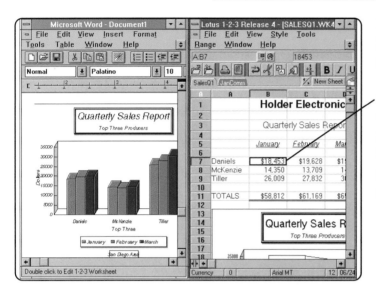

1. Click anywhere on the **1-2-3 worksheet** if it isn't already highlighted.

2. Click twice on **B7** on the worksheet. The cell will be surrounded by a black border. The current sales numbers for this cell will appear in the contents box.

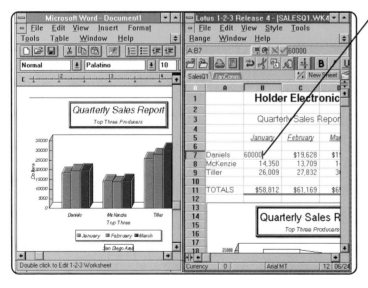

3. Press and hold the mouse button as you **drag** the cursor over **18,453**.

4. Type 60000.

5. Press the **Enter** key and watch the fun. Daniels' January column will automatically enlarge in both windows. The link works!

Notice that the Top Three chart reflects the change you made in the 1-2-3 spreadsheet.

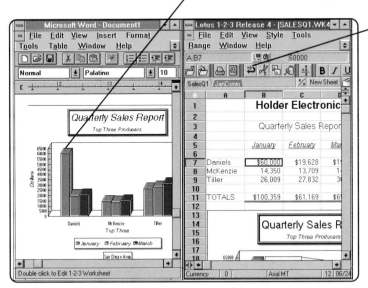

6. **Click** on the **Undo SmartIcon** in the 1-2-3 window to undo the change. The worksheet and the linked chart will return to their original versions.

Just for Fun!

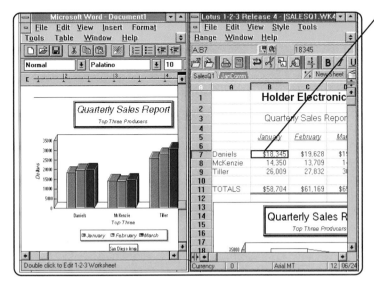

Try changing other numbers on the worksheet and watch the resulting changes in the word processing document chart.

If you are going to use the 1-2-3 worksheet to complete other chapters in this book, remember to change the numbers on the worksheet back to their original amounts.

MAXIMIZING LOTUS 1-2-3

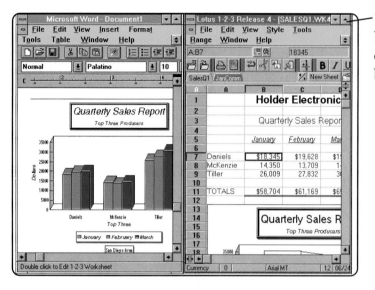

1. Click on the **Maximize button** (▲) on the right side of the title bar. 1-2-3 will become full size.

CLOSING THE WORD DOCUMENT

1. Click on the **Control menu box** (▭) to the left of the Lotus 1-2-3 title bar. A pull-down menu will appear.

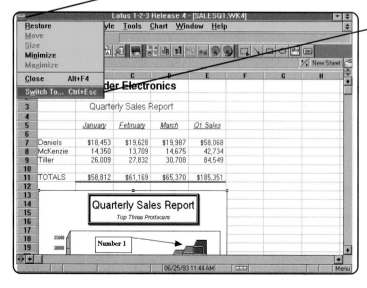

2. Click on **Switch To**. The Task List dialog box will appear.

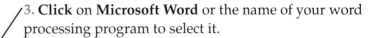

3. Click on **Microsoft Word** or the name of your word processing program to select it.

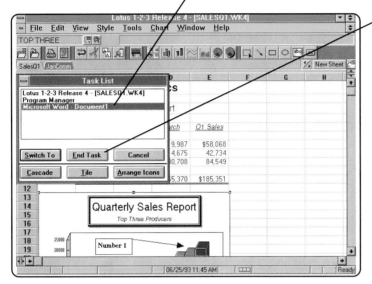

4. Click on **End Task**. The Microsoft Word save changes dialog box will appear.

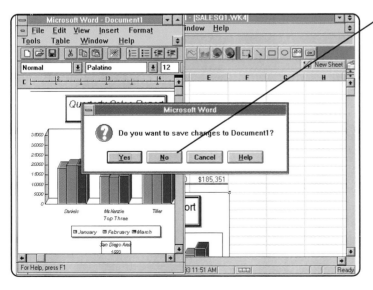

5. Click on **No**. The Word document will close. The 1-2-3 window will reappear.

MAXIMIZING PROGRAM MANAGER

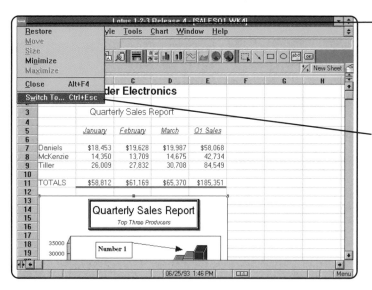

1. Click on the **Control menu box** (⊟) on the left side of the Lotus 1-2-3 title bar. A pull-down menu will appear.

2. Click on **Switch To**. The Task List dialog box will appear.

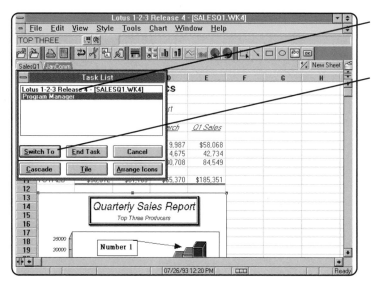

3. Click on **Program Manager**.

4. Click on **Switch To**. The group window will appear.

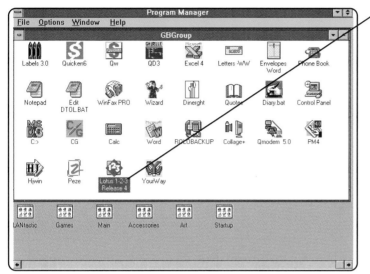

5. **Click twice** on the **Lotus 1-2-3 icon** to return to the program. The 1-2-3 SALESQ1 spreadsheet will reappear.

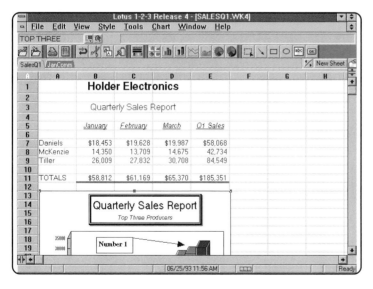

If you plan to go on to the next chapter now, leave the chart window as it is in this example.

Sealing and Protecting Worksheets

Computer security is increasingly a real concern for businesses in the 90s. Even at home, where the whole family shares the same computer, preventing accidental changes to a file can be a real challenge! Lotus 1-2-3 has several options to meet the security needs of most computer users. You can *seal* a file with a password. When a file is sealed, anyone can look at it but only those who know the password can make changes.

For a very private file, you can prevent anyone from even opening it by *protecting* it with a password. **Caution:** The problem with protecting a file with a password is that no one, even you, can open **that file** without the exact **password**. In this chapter, you will do the following:

❖ Seal a worksheet file so that it can be opened by others but cannot be changed without the correct password

❖ Protect a worksheet file so that only a person with the correct password can open it

❖ Remove seals and protections

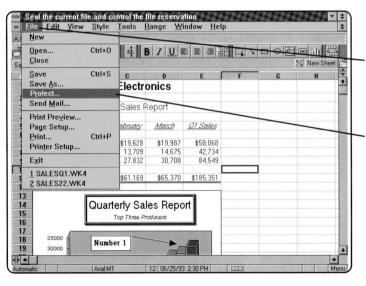

SEALING A FILE

1. **Click** on **File** in the menu bar. A pull-down menu will appear.

2. **Click** on **Protect**. The Protect dialog box will appear.

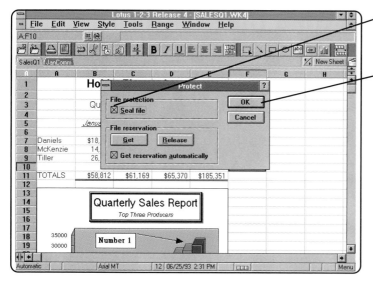

3. **Click** on **Seal file** to **place an** ✕ **in the box.**

4. **Click** on **OK**. The Set Password dialog box will appear.

5. **Type** a password in the **Password text box**. Each letter or number you type will show on the screen as an asterisk (*). A password can include up to fifteen characters in any combination. The password feature is case sensitive, so if you use a combination of upper- and lower-case letters, you must remember the exact combination.

6. **Press** the **Tab** key. The cursor will move to the Verify text box.

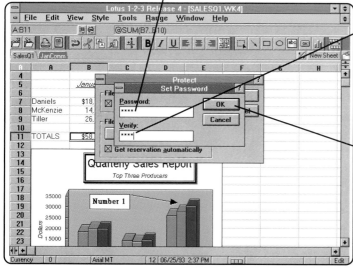

7. **Type** the same password again in the **Verify text box**. If you do not type the password exactly as you typed it in step 5, you will be prompted to begin again.

8. **Click** on **OK**. The SalesQ1.WK4 worksheet will reappear.

Testing the Sealed File Password Protection

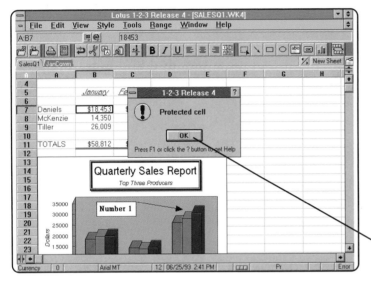

1. Click on cell **B7** to select it.

2. Type any number. The 1-2-3 Release 4 dialog box will appear, containing the message "Protected cell." This means that you "can look but not edit." In fact, no one can change this worksheet until you remove the password protection.

3. Click on **OK**. The dialog box will disappear.

Unsealing the Worksheet Password Protection

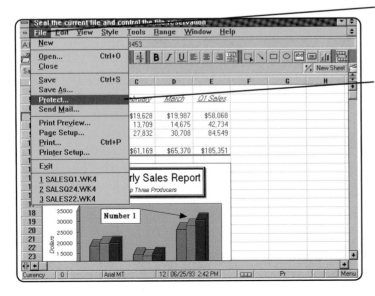

1. Click on **File** in the menu bar. A pull-down menu will appear.

2. Click on **Protect**. The Protect dialog box will appear.

3. Click on the **Seal file box** to **remove** the X.

4. Click on **OK**. The Get Password dialog box will appear.

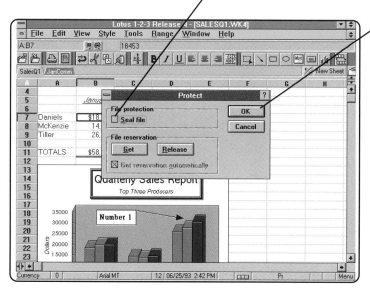

5. Type your password in the **Password text box**.

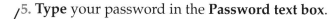

6. Click on **OK**. The SALESQ1.WK4 worksheet will appear. You can now make changes in it.

If you typed the wrong password, a 1-2-3 Release 4 dialog box with the message "Incorrect password" will appear. Click on OK, and then repeat in this section steps 1 to 5, entering the correct password. If you forgot the password, you are in deep fertilizer. You will have to re-create the file.

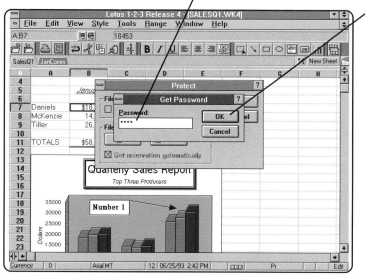

PREVENTING UNAUTHORIZED OPENING OF A WORKSHEET

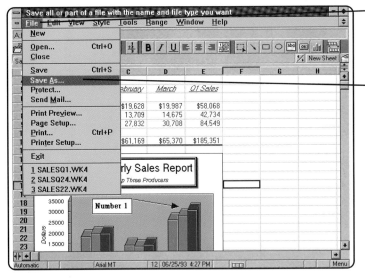

1. Click on **File** in the menu bar. A pull-down menu will appear.

2. Click on **Save As**. The Save As dialog box will appear.

3. Click on **With password** to place an ✕ in the box.

4. Click on **OK**. The File Save Options dialog box will appear.

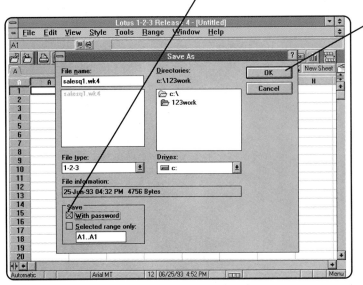

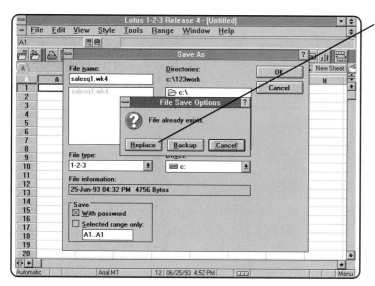

5. Click on **Replace**. The Set Password dialog box will appear. The cursor will be flashing in the Password text box.

6. Type a **password** in the **Password text box** and **press** the **Tab** key. The cursor will move to the Verify text box. (See step 5 in the section "Sealing a File" for rules on passwords.)

7. Type the same password again in the **Verify text box**. If you do not type the password exactly as you did in step 6, you will be prompted to begin again.

8. Click on **OK**. The SalesQ1.WK4 worksheet will reappear.

Testing the Password

In order to test whether or not the password option will prevent unauthorized opening of the worksheet, you must close the file and then reopen it.

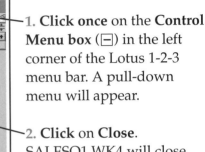

1. Click once on the **Control Menu box** (⊟) in the left corner of the Lotus 1-2-3 menu bar. A pull-down menu will appear.

2. Click on **Close**. SALESQ1.WK4 will close and a blank worksheet screen will appear.

3. Click on the **Open an Existing File SmartIcon**. The Open File dialog box will appear.

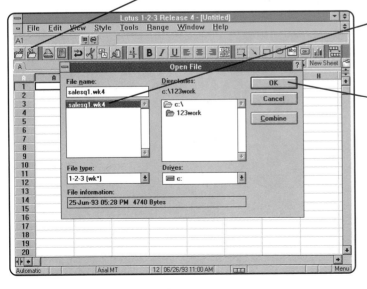

4. Click on **salesq1.wk4**. Salesq1.wk4 will move to the File Name text box.

5. Click on **OK**. The Get Password dialog box will appear.

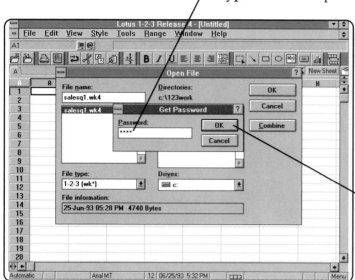

6. Type the correct password in the **Password text box**. (If you do not type the correct password, the file will not open and the 1-2-3 Release 4 dialog box will appear with the message "Incorrect password." In that case, click on OK. A blank screen will appear. Start over with step 1).

7. Click on **OK**. The SALESQ1.WK4 worksheet will appear.

Removing the Password

Because you must be in the file to remove a password, complete the previous section to open the password-protected file if you have not already done so. After you are in a protected file, removing a password is easy.

1. Click on **Fil**e in the menu bar. A pull-down menu will appear.

2. Click on **Save As**. The Save As dialog box will appear.

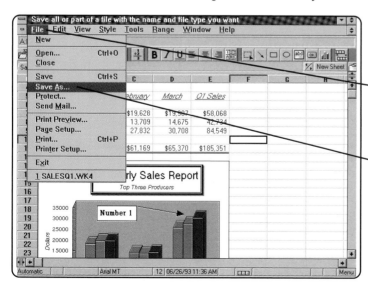

3. Click on **With password** to remove the X from the box.

4. Click on **OK**. The File Save Options dialog box will appear.

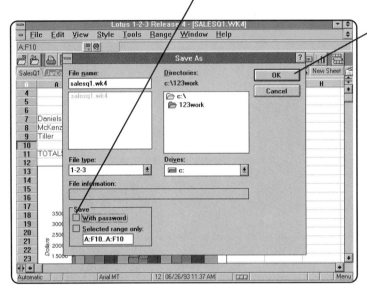

5. Click on **Replace**. The SALESQ1.WK4 worksheet will appear. The worksheet can now be opened by anyone.

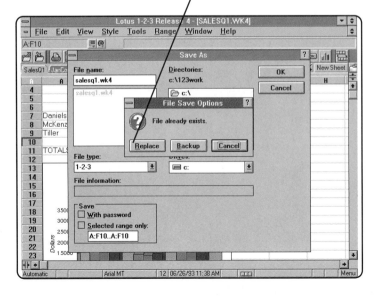

Caution: The problem with using passwords to prevent unauthorized entry is that no one can open that file without the exact password. That includes you!

We suggest you pick a password you know you will remember! You can use the same password on more than one file.

Converting Another Program's Worksheet to 1-2-3

Lotus has made converting a worksheet from another spreadsheet program, quite literally, as easy as 1-2-3. In this chapter, you will do the following:

❖ Open a worksheet from another program and convert it to a Lotus 1-2-3 for Windows worksheet

❖ Save the converted worksheet as a Lotus 1-2-3 for Windows file

OPENING A WORKSHEET FROM ANOTHER PROGRAM

To convert a spreadsheet from another program, such as Excel 4 or Symphony, you simply open the file. Lotus 1-2-3 does the rest!

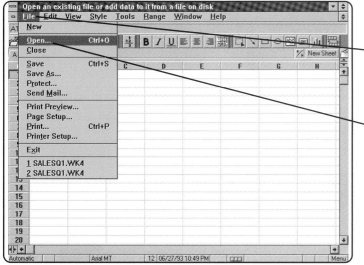

1. **Open** a new **worksheet**.

2. **Click** on **File** in the menu bar. A pull-down menu will appear.

3. **Click** on **Open**. The Open File dialog box will appear.

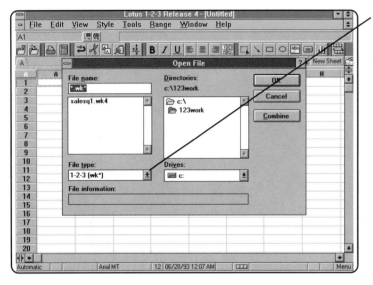

4. Click on the ⬇ on the **File Type text box**. A drop-down list of file types will appear.

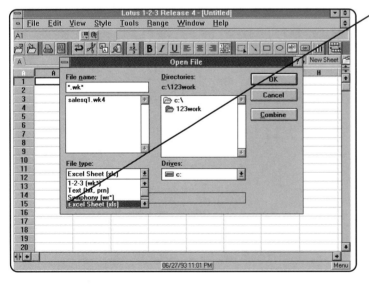

5. Click on **the type of file** you want to convert. It will appear in the file type text box. In this example, we are using Excel Sheet (xls).

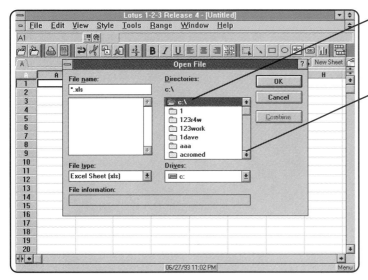

6. Click twice on **c:**. A list of all directories on the C drive will appear.

7. Click repeatedly on the ⬇ to **scroll down** the **list of directories** until you find the directory that contains the worksheet you want to convert. In this example, the file is in the Excelwrk directory.

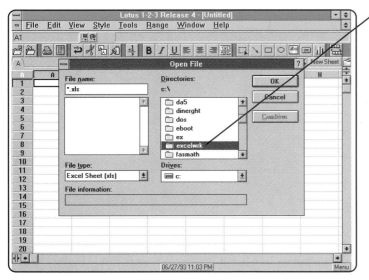

8. Click twice on the **directory name**. The files in the directory will appear in the File name list box on the left.

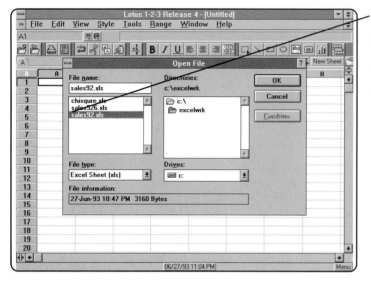

9. Click twice on the **file** you want to convert. The 1-2-3 Release 4 dialog box will appear with the message "File and/or extension converted."

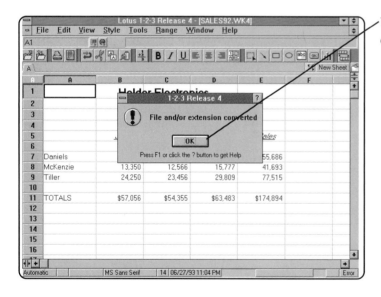

10. Click on **OK**. The newly converted file will appear.

Notice that the converted file already has the .WK4 extension for Lotus 1-2-3 for Windows.

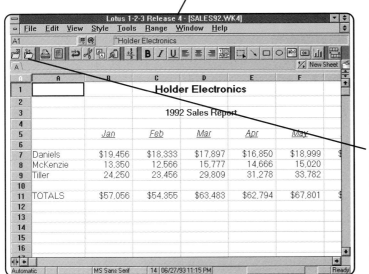

SAVING THE CONVERTED FILE

1. **Click** on the **Save SmartIcon**. Your screen won't change, but the file is now saved as a Lotus 1-2-3 worksheet. The original file (in this case, an Excel 4 file) will remain intact.

Note: You may have to change the fonts to get the newly converted worksheet to look the way your other 1-2-3 sheets do.

Moving and Sizing SmartIcons

If you find the SmartIcons just a little too small to see comfortably, 1-2-3 has just the thing for you. You can make the SmartIcons considerably larger. You can even change the position of the SmartIcons. In this chapter, you will do the following:

❖ Change the position of the SmartIcons

❖ Make the SmartIcons larger

MOVING THE SmartIcons

You can move the SmartIcons to the left, right, or bottom of the worksheet. You can even choose a floating position, which allows you to place them anywhere. You can change the SmartIcons at any time, but this example will start with a new worksheet on the screen.

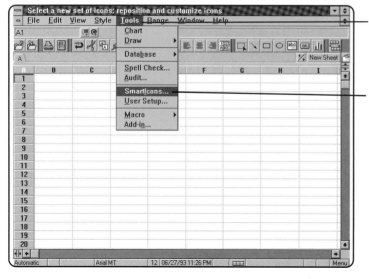

1. **Click** on **Tools** in the menu bar. A pull-down menu will appear.

2. **Click** on **SmartIcons**. The SmartIcons dialog box will appear.

3. Click on ⬇ to the right of the Positions text box. A drop-down list will appear.

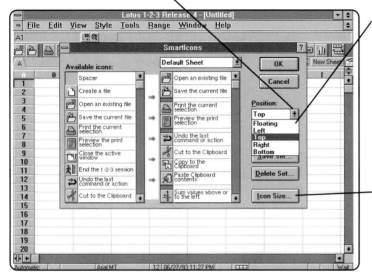

4. Click on **Floating**. The list will close and Floating will appear in the text box.

SIZING THE SMARTICONS

1. While you are in the SmartIcons dialog box, **click** on **Icon Size**. The Icon Size dialog box will appear.

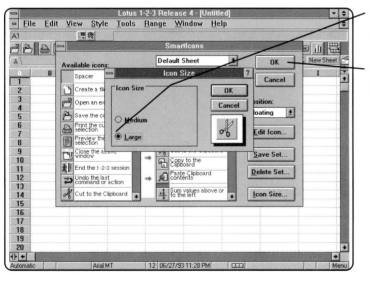

2. Click on **Large** to insert a dot in the circle.

3. Click on **OK**. The Icon Size dialog box will close.

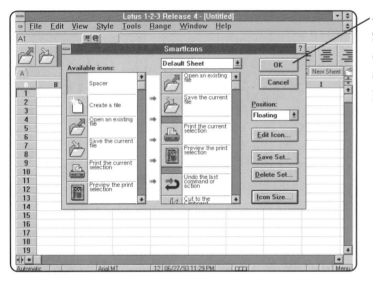

4. Click on **OK**. The SmartIcons dialog box will close. The SmartIcons will appear near the bottom of your screen.

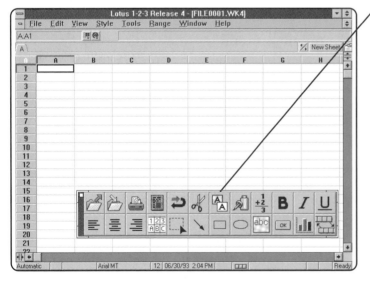

If you do not see a double line of SmartIcons, go to the next section, where you will increase the size of the SmartIcon bar so that you can see them all.

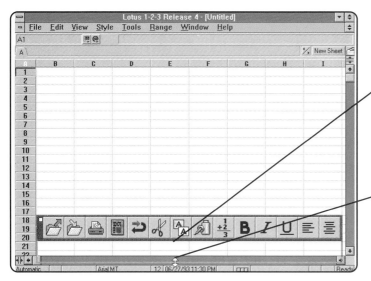

ENLARGING THE ICON BAR

1. Place the **mouse pointer** in the **middle of the bottom border** of the Icon bar. The pointer will change to a white two-headed arrow.

2. Press and hold the mouse button and **drag** the border **down** to a position that will double the space for the icons.

3. Release the mouse button. All the SmartIcons in this set are now visible.

You can change these back to the standard size and position by repeating the steps in this chapter and clicking on Top position and Medium size.

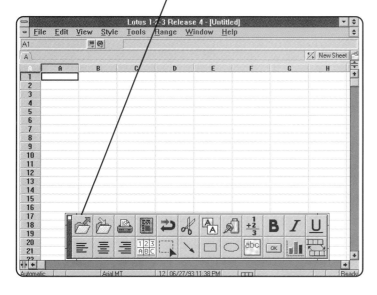

WHAT NEXT?

There are many exciting features of 1-2-3 left to explore. We hope this introduction has given you an understanding of its capabilities. We hope, also, that you have gained confidence in your ability to master its complexities.

Experiment! Have fun!

Program Manager

Part VI: Appendix

Installing Lotus 1-2-3 for Windows | Page 220

Installing Lotus 1-2-3 for Windows

In this appendix, you will do the following:

❖ Make backup copies of your Lotus 1-2-3 disks

❖ Install Lotus 1-2-3

❖ Install Adobe Type Manager 2.5

BACK UP YOUR LOTUS 1-2-3 DISKS!

Before you start, make certain that you have six formatted disks handy. This example shows how to copy disks using Windows File Manager. (If you have another file manager program or copy program, such as QDOS of CopyQM, you can use it to back up the original 1-2-3 disks).

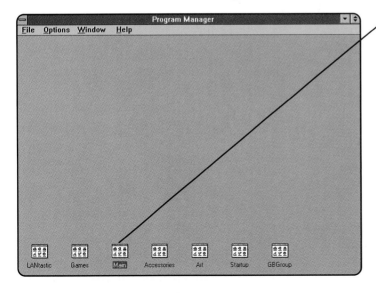

1. Click twice on the **Main group icon**. The Main group window will appear.

2. **Click twice** on the **File Manager icon**. The file Manager window will appear. Your File Manager icon may be in a different spot than you see here.

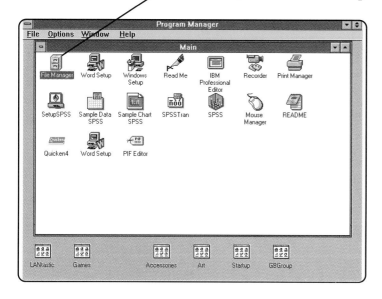

3. **Click** on **Disk** in the menu bar. A pull-down menu will appear.

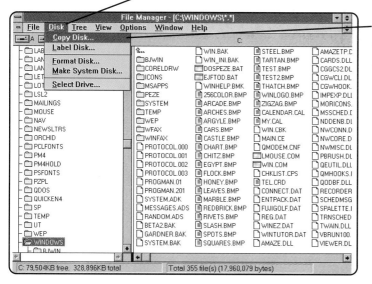

4. **Click** on **Copy Disk**. The Copy Disk dialog box will appear.

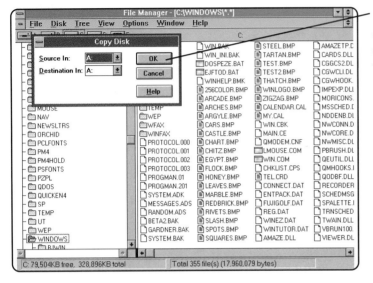

5. Click on **OK** if you are copying to drive A. The Confirm Copy Disk dialog box will appear on your screen.

(If you are using drive B, **click** on the ⬇ to the right of the Source In box. A drop-down list will appear. Click on B. Repeat these steps for the Destination In box.)

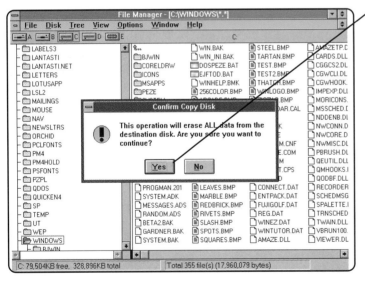

6. Click on **Yes**. The Copy Disk dialog box will appear.

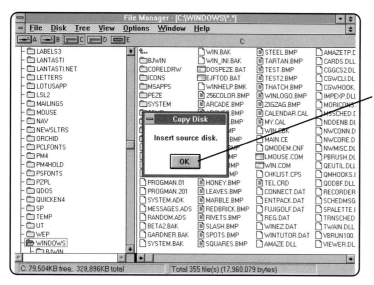

7. Insert the **Lotus 1-2-3 disk 1 (install)** into drive A (or B).

8. Click on **OK**. The Copy Disk dialog box will appear.

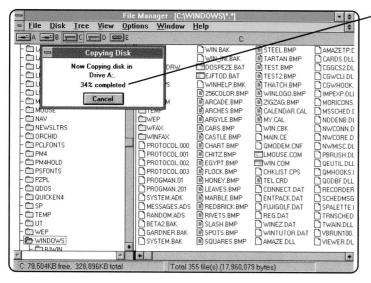

The Copying Disk dialog box will tell you the percentage of the copying that is being done. When the copying is completed, the Copy Disk dialog box will appear.

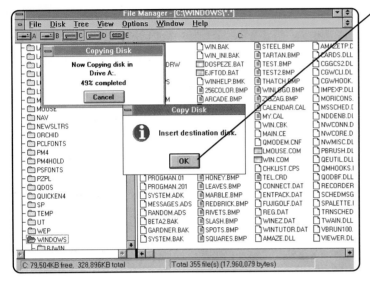

9. **Click** on **OK**.

10. **Remove** the **"copying" disk** from drive A.

11. **Insert** the **Copy to (destination) disk** into drive A.

The Copying Disk dialog box will appear again and show you the progress of the copying process. When disk #1 is finished copying, the original File Manager screen will appear.

Repeat steps 3 through 9 to copy disks 2 through 6. If you want to install the latest version of Adobe Type Manager (ATM), copy the ATM disk also.

EXITING FILE MANAGER

1. **Click** on **File** in the menu bar. A pull-down menu will appear.

2. **Click** on **Exit**. File Manager will close. Your original screen will appear.

INSTALLING LOTUS 1-2-3

If you have a screen saver, be sure to turn it off before beginning the installation process.

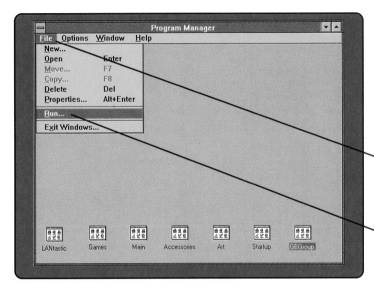

1. **Insert** your **backup** copy of 1-2-3 **Disk 1 (install)** in Drive A (or B). Be certain to use your backup copies during the installation. Store original disks in a safe place.

2. **Click** on **File** in the menu bar. A pull-down menu will appear.

3. **Click** on **Run**. The Run dialog box will appear.

Notice that the cursor is flashing in the Command Line text box. It will disappear when you start typing.

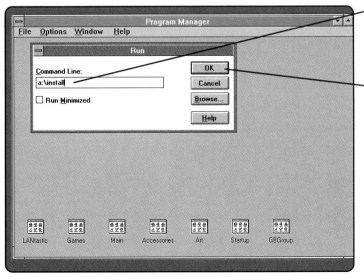

4. **Type a:\install** (or b:\install) in the Command Line text box.

5. **Click** on **OK**. The hourglass will appear briefly along with a Please Wait message box that says, "Install is copying its working files to your hard disk."

The Welcome to Install dialog box will appear.

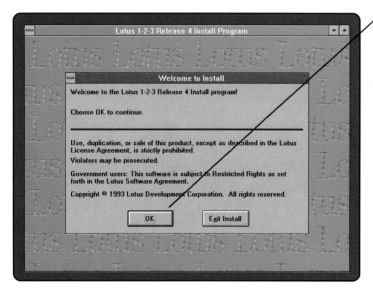

6. **Click** on **OK**. The Name and Company dialog box will appear.

Notice that the cursor is flashing in the Name text box. When you start typing, it will disappear.

7. **Type** your **full name** in the Enter your name text box and then **press** the **Tab** key to move the cursor to the organization text box.

8. **Type** the **name of your organization**, if applicable, in the organization text box.

9. **Click** on **OK**. The Confirm Names dialog box will appear.

10. Click on **Yes** if the information is correct. A message saying, "Saving initialization information" will appear briefly on your screen. Next, the 1-2-3 Main Menu dialog box will appear.

If the information is not correct, **click** on **No**. The previous dialog box will reappear. After making your corrections, **click** on **OK** (see step 9) to return to this dialog box and complete step 10.

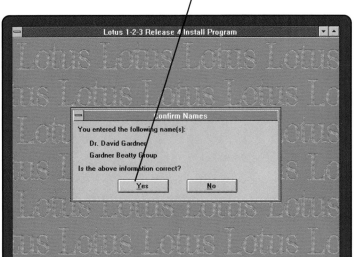

11. Click on **Install 1-2-3**. The Type of Installation dialog box will appear.

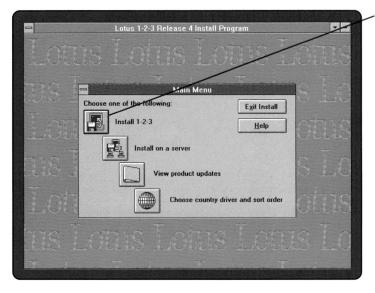

12. Click on **Default Install** to follow the procedures in this book. A Please Wait message box will appear briefly that says "Scanning the drives on your system." Then the Directory dialog box will appear.

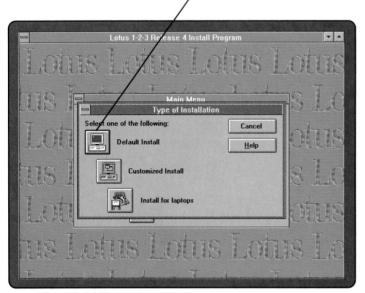

If you are an experienced 1-2-3 user, you may **click** on the **Customized Install option**. The Customized Install procedure will not be illustrated here. If you have a laptop, **click** on **Install for Laptops**. The procedure will not be illustrated here.

13. Click on **OK**. The Confirm Directory dialog box will appear.

Note: If you want to install 1-2-3 on another drive (drive D:, for example), click on the down arrow to the right of the available drives. A drop-down list of drives will appear.

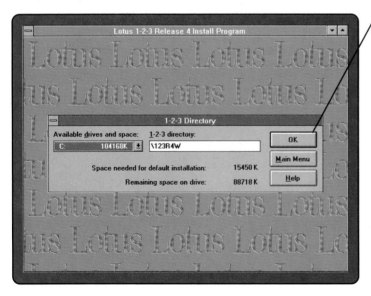

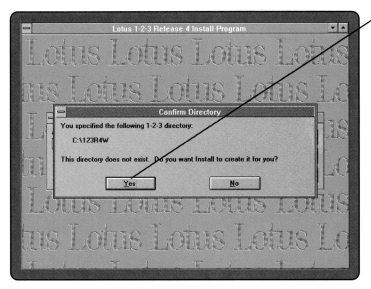

14. Click on **Yes**. The Lotus Common Directory dialog box will appear.

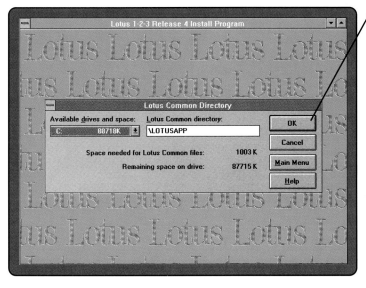

15. Click on **OK**. The Confirm Directory dialog box will appear.

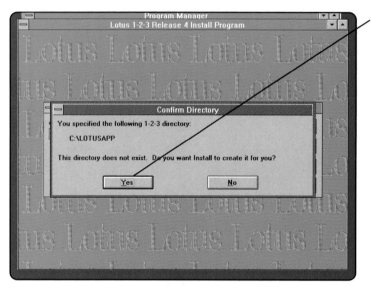

16. Click on **Yes**. Several message boxes will appear, and then the Transferring Files dialog box will appear as 1-2-3 begins copying files from disk 1 (install).

Notice that 1-2-3 shows you the percentage of files being copied from the disk in drive A. It also shows you the percentage of all the files on all the 1-2-3 installation disks copied.

Note: This may take a while, so be patient. (The percent value may seem to stick around certain numbers. Don't worry; that's a normal part of the process.)

When 1-2-3 finishes copying the files from disk 1, the 1-2-3 for Windows Install Program dialog box will appear.

17. **Remove disk 1** from drive A and **insert disk 2** in drive A.

18. **Click** on **OK**. The Transferring Files dialog box will reappear. 1-2-3 will begin copying files on disk 2.

19. **Repeat** steps **17 and 18** for disks 2 through 5.

As soon as disk 5 has been copied, an Installation Finished dialog box will appear.

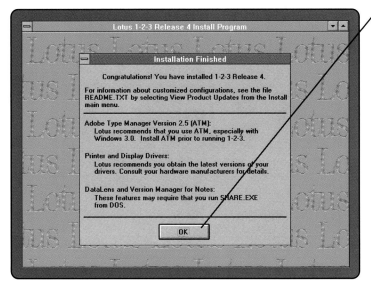

20. **Click** on **OK**. The Take the Guided tour message box will appear.

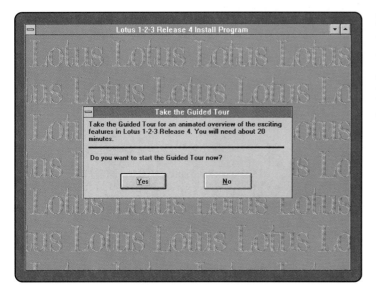

21. If you would like to start the Guided tour, a 20-minute tutorial, **click** on **Yes**. If not, **click** on **No** to continue. The Main menu dialog box will appear.

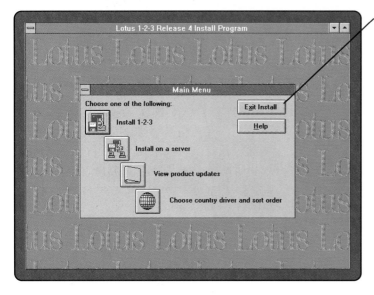

22. Click on **Exit Install**. After you have completed this installation, the Lotus Application's group window will appear. (Don't forget to take the last disk out of drive A).

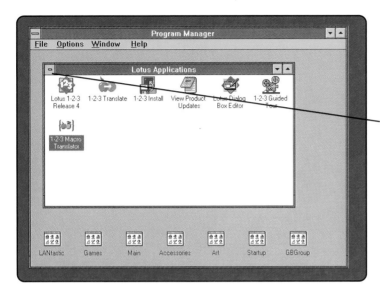

CLOSING THE GROUP WINDOW

1. Click twice on the **Control menu box** ([−]) in the Lotus Applications title bar. The Lotus Application's group window will appear as an icon at the bottom of your screen.

Because windows allows for tremendous customization; the group icons at the bottom of your screen will probably be different from the ones you see here.

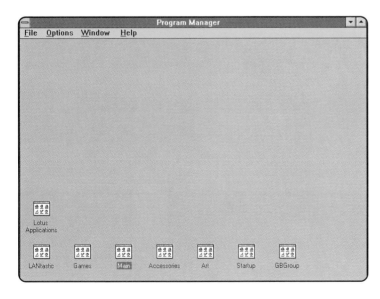

According to Lotus 1-2-3, you do not have to reinstall Adobe Type Manager, version 2.5, if you already have this version. However, in our testing, even though we had machines with 2.5 already installed, we found that 1-2-3 simply works better if you reinstall. If you have an older version of Adobe Type Manager, you must install version 2.5.

INSTALLING ADOBE TYPE MANAGER

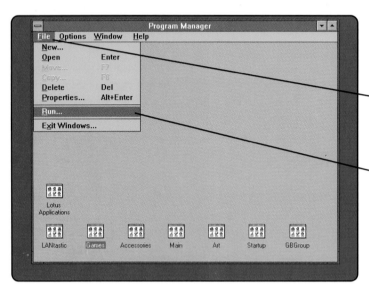

1. **Insert** the **Adobe Type Manager disk** in drive A (or B.)

2. **Click** on **File** in the menu bar. A pull-down menu will appear.

3. **Click** on **Run**. The Run dialog box will appear. The cursor will be flashing in the Command Line text box.

4. **Type a:** (or b:) in the Command Line text box.

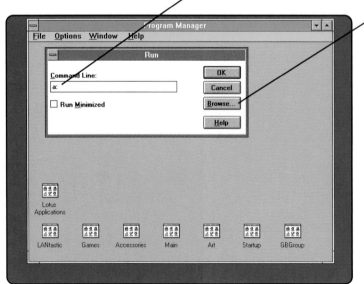

5. **Click** on **Browse**. The Browse dialog box will appear.

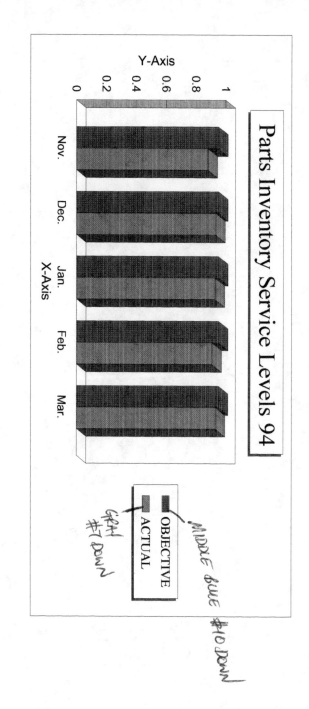

6. Click on **install.exe** in the file list box. Install.exe will appear in the File Name text box.

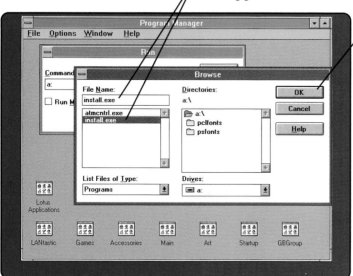

7. Click on **OK**. The Run dialog box will appear again. A:\INSTALL.EXE will appear in the Command Line text box.

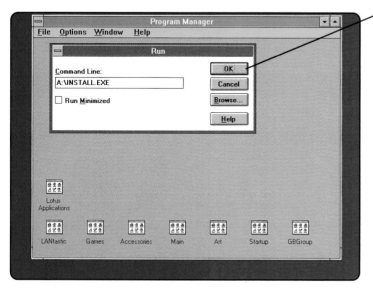

8. Click on **OK**. An ATM Installer dialog box will appear.

If you have an older version of Adobe type Manager, the messages in the two dialog boxes on this page will be somewhat different. In any event, bear with us . . . and keep on clicking!

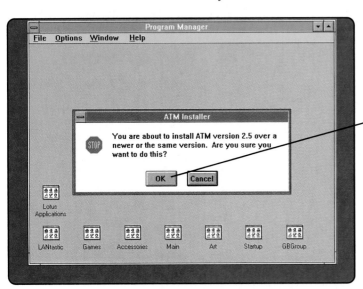

9. **Click** on **OK**. Another ATM dialog box will appear.

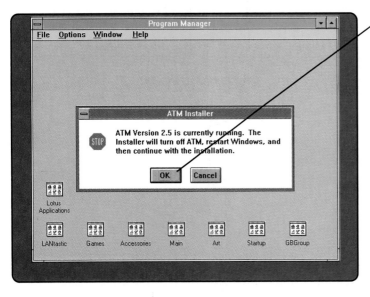

10. **Click** on **OK**. The screen will go blank for a few seconds, and then the Program Manager screen will reappear, rather faded-looking at first. Don't fret; you did nothing wrong.

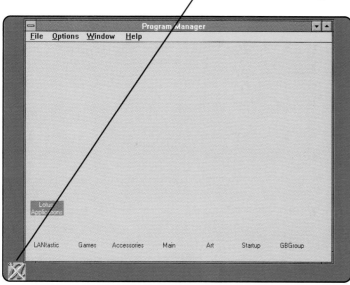

Notice that, as Program Manager reappears, the ATM icon will show with an ✕ through it for a brief moment before disappearing.

Next, notice that an hourglass will appear for a while and then the ATM Installer dialog box will appear.

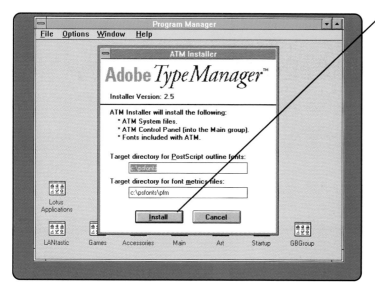

11. **Click** on **Install**. An ATM Installer message box will appear.

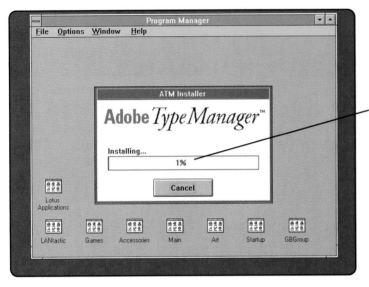

This ATM Installer message box will be on your screen for quite a while as the installer does its work.

It will keep you posted on its progress, however, as you wait for the next event. Eventually, another ATM Installer dialog box will appear in the foreground.

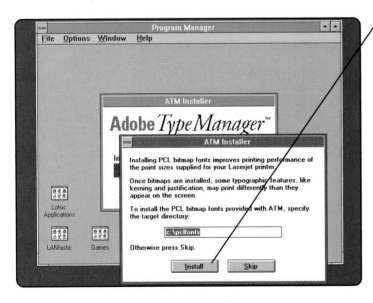

12. **Click** on **Install**. The ATM Installer dialog box will disappear and the ATM Installer message box will come to the foreground.

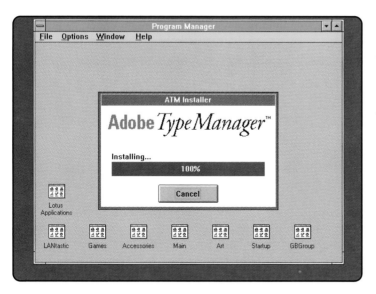

This message box will hang around a while longer. When it reaches 100%, ATM 2.5 is installed at last. The last ATM Installer dialog box will appear as shown in the next example.

RESTARTING WINDOWS

Warning: It is very important that you restart windows now in order for the new Adobe Type Manager to take effect.

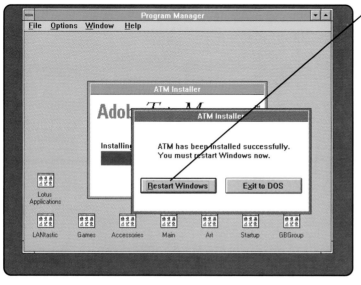

1. **Click** on **Restart Windows**. Your screen will become dark and eventually Windows will reappear.

You're now ready to begin using 1-2-3. Enjoy!

Index

X

X-axis. *See* Bar charts

Y

Y-axis. *See* Bar charts

Z

Zoom feature, 116-117
  customizing zoom percentage,
    117-118